Life and sport in China

by Oliver G. Ready

AUTHOR'S NOTE

The British public is greatly handicapped in forming an intelligent appreciation of happenings in China by a lack of that initial experience which can only be gained by residence in the country.

In this little work I have endeavoured to place before readers a sketch of things as I saw them, and to convey to their minds an idea of how Europeans live there, of their amusements, of their work, and of those things which are matters of daily interest to them, so that my book may serve as a kind of preface to that enthralling volume, the current history of China, as it is daily revealed in the press, in magazines and in learned works.

While confining myself herein to the lighter side of narrative, I am not unconscious of those intricate problems and deep studies connected with the Far East, but to which profound research and matured judgment must be applied, though information thereon, even when collected and published, would appeal mostly to the narrow circle of experts on matters Chinese.

The vast Empire of China with its hundreds of millions of toiling slaves, with its old, old civilisation reaching back for untold years prior to the dawn of history in the West, with its manners and customs so worn into the national character that they almost form the character itself, with its fertile plains, its sandy deserts, its lofty mountains, its mighty rivers, its torrid heat and arctic cold, its devastating floods, its cruel famines and loathsome epidemics, represents a mass, the contemplation of which staggers the mind and makes one ask, "What is Europe trying to do here? Does she hope to conquer, to change or to purify?"

After a residence of twelve years in various parts of the country I instinctively feel that while military occupation by the Great Powers may be possible, not only is China in a sense unconquerable, but that she is eminently a conquering nation, though not by clash of arms. Insidiously, remorselessly and viciously she will subdue apostles of the West who are sent to her, and unless persistently restrained will overflow into adjacent lands and conquer there by cheap labour and unremitting toil.

For the photographs I am indebted to the generosity of Mrs T. Child, as well as to T.T.H. Ferguson, A.J.E. Allen, Carlos Cabral and the late H. Hall, Esquires.

CONTENTS

=Bund.= The embankment or quay of a concession.

=Concession.= A strip of land conceded by China to another Power exclusively for the residences of foreigners.

=Chit.= Any letter or note, also an I.O.U.

=Chop chop.= Quickly. Hurry up.

=Compradore.= Chinese agent or partner.

=Coolie.= Chinese labourer.

=Cumshaw.= A tip or present.

=European.= In China this word is equally applicable to Americans.

=Foreigner.= European or American in China.

=Gingall.= Heavy muzzle-loading musket requiring two men to carry and fire it.

=Han, Children of.= Chinese.

=Kowtow.= To make obeisance by striking the head on the ground.

=Lowdah.= Sailing-master.

=Mafoo.= Groom.

=Native.= Chinese.

=Out-port.= Any treaty port except Shanghai, and Hongkong.

=Papico.= Junk from Ningpo, shaped aft like a duck.

=Pow.= To gallop.

=Praia Grande.= Esplanade facing sea.

=Pumelo.= A coarse fruit resembling an enormous orange.

=Punkah.= Large fan suspended from ceiling for ventilating room.

=Ricksha.= Small gig drawn by a coolie, who plies it for hire.

=Runner.= Official underling. Police agent.

=Sai.= Here I am. A word used by servants combining Sir and Lai, to come.

=Samli.= A fish resembling salmon.

=Sampan.= Small native boat.

=Samshu.= Spirit distilled from rice or millet.

=Settlement.= Where Europeans have settled on a limited strip of Chinese territory.

=Shroff.= Chinese accountant, cashier and banker.

=Squeeze.= Recognised cheating.

=Sycee Shoes.= Rough lumps of silver cast in shape of China-woman's small shoe or of half-globe.

=Tiffin.= Luncheon.

=Treaty-port.= Any port opened by treaty to foreign trade.

=Waler.= Horse from New South Wales.

=Westerner.= European or American.

=Yulow.= A scull worked over the stern.

=Zacousca.= Russian appetiser or snack taken before meals.

Life and Sport in China

CHAPTER I

ANGLO-CHINESE LIFE

Anglo-Chinese life is a sealed book to most people at home, who, if they ever think about it at all, do so with minds adversely biassed by ignorance of the conditions, a hazy idea of intense heat, and a remembrance of cruel massacres.

"Going to China" always elicits looks and exclamations of astonishment at so rash an undertaking, but which the stock questions as to whether we eat with chopsticks, whether it is not always unbearably hot, and whether we like the Chinese, explain as disquietude arising from the idea of encountering "evils that we know not of."

Our early business relations with the Chinese were conducted at Canton, to which port opium in particular was shipped direct from India, but owing to the hostility of Chinese officials towards British merchants and the legitimate expansion of their trade, quarrels were frequent, culminating in the so-called Opium War of 1840-42, resulting in the acquisition by us of the small, barren island of Hongkong, and the opening to foreign trade of five ports, including Canton and Shanghai, at all of which small plots of land some half a mile square were set apart for the exclusive residence of foreigners generally but of Englishmen in particular. Disputes, however, did not cease, so that twenty years later England and France in co-operation, attacked China, and wrung from her the right of foreign ministers accredited to the Chinese court to reside at Peking, and also that additional ports should be opened to foreign trade, with a plot of land at each for residential purposes.

The treaties following on these two wars have since been supplemented by other treaties opening still more ports, at some of which also adjoining plots of land have likewise been conceded, and our position in China to-day is founded on the accumulated result of these various agreements, which, above all things, guarantee us exterritoriality or exemption from Chinese jurisdiction, so that Europeans for whatever misdemeanours, are amenable only to their own consuls.

There are now about thirty treaty-ports, most of them having these residential plots or concessions some of which, however, have never been taken up and built on, but where they have been, although leased from the Chinese Government at nominal rents, they are to all intents and purposes little detached portions of the British Empire, kept scrupulously clean and in perfect order, where natives are not allowed to dwell, but where Europeans of all nationalities live in security and comfort.

In each of them resides a British consul, who represents his Government vis-

?vis the Chinese and foreign officials, and who holds the position of magistrate in relation to his own nationals. An English doctor also is generally in practice at all, except the very smallest, ports.

In many instances walls have been built round these concessions, the gateways in which can be bolted and barred at night to keep out the natives, a good system of drainage introduced, wide roads laid out and lighted, public seats placed in pleasant spots facing the water, trees planted, palatial houses built with gardens attached, a church constructed, clubs founded, billiard-tables and other insignia of Western luxury imported, a municipal council elected for managing local affairs, and a force of native police or Indian Sikhs raised, with which, under English superintendents, to maintain order in our streets.

Other countries, notably France, have similar settlements, though far less numerous, but I shall herein refer exclusively to our own.

Off the frontage or bund is frequently moored a line of hulks connected with the shore by pontoons, and which in their day were probably the finest ocean liners afloat, but now, worn out and dismantled, serve as floating warehouses, alongside which steamers come to discharge and load cargo. At other places vessels drop anchor in mid-stream, while between them and the various jetties large cargo boats constantly pass to and fro laden with merchandise, to be quickly shipped or landed by gangs of chattering coolies.

Everywhere the foreshore is always crowded with a fleet of native junks, displaying half mast be it a bundle of wood, a rice measure or a coal scoop, to show that their cargoes consisting of wood, rice, coal, etc., are for sale.

Either just on the concession, by permission of the consul, or in Chinatown immediately outside, are two or three general stores and butchers' shops, run by either Chinese, Parsees or Japanese, especially to supply the foreign community with groceries, bread, meat and other daily requisites.

No one carries money in his pocket, for the Europeans being but few in number are well known by sight, and any purchase is made by signing an I.O.U., or chit, for the amount necessary in dollars or cents. At the club you call for say two sherries and one bamboo (half sherry, half vermouth) and the waiter brings them, together with a small chit-book in which he has already written down your order in pencil, and this, after inspection, you simply sign or initial, when it is torn out and dropped into the till and you see no more of it until the end of the month, when your club bill comes in, supported by all the chits you have signed.

For the offertory, pencils and pieces of paper are distributed about the church, so that the congregation may easily write chits, which are folded up and dropped into the bag, to be presented at your house next day by the church coolie for payment. This system, though very convenient, is apt to prove something of a trap, for signing a chit is so much easier, and the amount appears to be so much less than if paying in hard cash, that when the monthly total is made up you are at first inclined to believe there must be some mistake; but alas! careful verification too plainly shows that you have signed for more than you had any idea of.

Amongst Europeans the currency employed is the silver dollar, now worth about one shilling and sevenpence though formerly rated at five shillings, together with a subsidiary coinage of fifty, twenty, ten and five-cent silver pieces, as well as coppers of one and two cents each.

The Chinese standard of value in universal use throughout the Empire is copper cash. A cash is about the size of a shilling and equivalent to one eighth of a farthing in value. Through the centre of each coin is a square hole large enough to admit a thick string. It is usual to thread cash, first into bundles of one hundred, each bundle being about the size and shape of a sausage, and then for ten bundles to be strung together in pairs, so that the full string of a thousand cash almost exactly corresponds to a double string of ten sausages. The value of this full string is about half-a-crown, and owing to its great weight is usually carried slung over the shoulder.

The tael, pronounced tale, is not a coin at all, but means simply an ounce (of silver). There are many kinds of taels, each of a different value according to the purity or touch of the silver, which is chiefly determined by the locality in which the metal is mined.

When a Chinaman sells native produce to a European he always keeps in mind its value in cash, and wants a corresponding value in dollars or taels, whatever the price of silver may happen to be. The same with wages of all kinds; the amount required in each case is based on what each individual requires in cash.

The whole monetary system, or rather lack of system, complicated by numberless local banks, each with its own issue of paper money, is so bewildering that European householders seldom bother about anything beyond dollars and cents, to which standard, for their especial benefit, all others are reduced, though always at a certain loss in the exchange.

Some of these concessions, which are in reality little English towns, have greatly prospered since their inauguration and are now centres of voluminous and increasing trade; but others, belying their initial prosperity, have stagnated, and appear to be gradually slipping back to the Chinese, who, in contravention of treaty ordinances, have been allowed to acquire property on them and reside there in rapidly-increasing numbers.

The thriving settlement of Shanghai, which is situated near the mouth of the River Yangtse, and which possesses a foreign population of six or seven thousand, may be considered the metropolis of other treaty-ports in the northern half of the Empire, or, as they are generally called, "out-ports"; while the British colony of Hongkong stands in the same relation to out-ports in the south.

Hongkong has now no connection whatever with China, being entirely a British possession, and has been converted from a barren rock to a most lovely, thriving and important commercial town and naval base, and is the greatest triumph of British enterprise and material civilisation that I know of.

Nearly all these out-ports are in telegraphic communication with either Shanghai or Hongkong, and through them with the outside world, while the postal service is conducted by means of coast and river steamers which, plying regularly with passengers and cargo, have bases in these two emporiums, so that in whatever port you reside your thoughts and your interests are daily and directly concerned with either one or the other. From them come the daily newspapers, arriving, maybe, several days after date of issue, but still fresh reading for those in distant places. From them come the gun-boats which, besides protection, bring the welcome society of jovial naval men, and from them come commercial travellers with assortments of hats, boots, guns, clothes and other necessaries; while to them we go to embark for home, or, when in need of a social holiday, to chip off the rust of out-port seclusion, until eventually we look to them for many of our creature comforts, and through them, as through a window, to the world beyond.

Existence at both Shanghai and Hongkong is surrounded with so many Western accessories in the shape of good houses, electric light, excellent roads, horses and carriages, bands in public gardens and hourly telegrams, that life at an out-port, while at times very monotonous, is frequently more interesting, for there, being less overshadowed by the pleasure of foreign society, you may come into closer touch with things Chinese, so that if the study of a people the most antiquated and wonderful under the sun has attractions for any, this, together with the many facilities for the enjoyment of sport and outdoor life, should be sufficient to bring occasional contentment to even the most despondent.

From the extreme north to the extreme south, and from the sea to the mean west, that is, along the coast line and up the River Yangtse for fourteen hundred miles to Chungking, these nests of British enterprise adhere like barnacles to China's stolid bulk, dominating her vast trade with other countries, appearing as bright oases in the desert of Eastern heathendom and unfriendliness, and ranging in numerical importance from say thirty to five hundred Europeans, in accordance with the amount of shipping which flows through them and is their very life-blood.

Much depends on the residents themselves whether social life in these miniature colonies is to be very pleasant or only a deadly monotony. Nearly every man who comes out from home has been selected from among his fellows for some particular superiority. Either he is smart in business, has health and physique to withstand the extremes of climate to which he may be subjected, is clever and has gained his appointment in competitive examination, or he may have all these qualities combined; anyhow, he is a picked man, above the average all round, and as such has a corresponding force of character.

A number of such men being thrown together in a small place either co-operate and become fast friends, their wives and children, if they have any, following suit, when existence is rendered charming, or, on the other hand, with their marked individualities and business rivalries they may quarrel, in which case the best thing is to forego all hopes of social pleasures and wrap yourself up in your own content. A quarrelsome port provides an amusing study for a short time, but after that, especially during the depressing dampness of the rainy season when it is too wet to go out, life becomes very monotonous and irritating, for the space being so limited you are continually brought face to face with people who are on bad terms and who try to attach you to their side. Trivial jealousies, mythical slights and insignificant nothings which would pass unnoticed in a larger world here assume such alarming proportions that the club languishes owing to numerous resignations, few attend church because one of the rival faction plays the organ, and the evening promenade beneath the trees along the bund is transformed from a pleasant family gathering into a funereal procession.

In pleasing contrast is a nice port, where people pull together, where good-fellowship and hospitality make one feel like the member of a large family, where you walk into the house of your neighbour, smoke his cigars and drink his whisky, brought to you while reclining in a long chair on the verandah with the punkah swinging lazily over you, waiting for the master's return. This is done with the pleasurable knowledge that your friend would naturally instal himself in your house under like circumstances. Here is real charm. Think, too, of the outdoor life, of those lovely evenings when the air is soft and warm, the moon at full and of a size never seen in England, when a party of us would sail out on the lake, drop anchor and dine in the cool breeze, and after cigars and coffee would sail on again, singing songs that carried us back to days of yore and bringing a sad yet sweet strain into thoughts and voices as we glided over the moonlit waters.

Spring and autumn bring the two great events of the year--the races.

Many ports have a capital race-course, which is always circular in shape, enclosing what are generally the grounds of the recreation club, while almost every sporting man trains a pony or two, which he frets and fumes over in a style that would not bemean a Newmarket turf magnate. Weeks before the meeting, increasing in intensity as the time shortens and decreasing slowly as the event recedes, the talk is purely of ponies, ponies, ponies--until the non-racing man droops and turns away, but without daring to utter one single word of protest against the prevailing epidemic of pony talk. Race lotteries at the club afford great excitement to the betting men, when the knowing ones make books which in the end leave them considerably to the bad, while those who know nothing rejoice with the joy of fools, thinking that to their own perspicuity is due the roll of dollars which wanton luck has thrust upon them.

On the actual race days, of which there are generally two, with a third or off-day tacked on, things reach a climax. All business is curtailed or altogether suspended. Everyone wears colours, either his own or those of a friend, and at eleven o'clock the ladies are driven to the course in state by happy owners of various nondescript vehicles furbished up for the occasion. Everyone knows everyone else, the names of ponies entered have been household words for weeks, while their supposed merits are open secrets, the jockeys are personal friends, the weather is bright and warm, the ladies wear their smartest dresses, the course is kept and order maintained with the aid of bluejackets from the gun-boat in port, while her drum and fife band or nigger troupe renders selections of varied merits. A race over, the successful owner and jockey are seized and carried shoulder high to the bar behind the grand-stand, where winners and losers alike have preceded them to secure a glass of champagne at the owner's expense, with which to drink his health and show a befitting sense of joy at the victory which has just been achieved.

An excellent champagne lunch is served in the grand-stand, and presided over by the clerk of the course, who, by virtue of his exalted office, ranks high in the community, when suitable toasts are proposed and cordially honoured, followed by an adjournment to the paddock for a stroll and a smoke, after which attention is again claimed for the business of the afternoon's racing.

Riding is usually well to the fore, and on an afternoon parties of ladies with attendant cavaliers trot down the reach by the river and gallop home across the plain, or wend along the beach, walking their ponies in the salt water.

For the sportsman game in abundance generally lies within reach, and nothing of its kind is more delightful than an afternoon with the spring snipe, or a shooting trip of a few days in company with a kindred spirit.

Tennis is still a favourite amusement during summer months, and garden-parties, comprising almost the whole community, meet frequently, be it on the club grounds or at private houses, when those who do not play come to watch and chat while partaking of ices and other refreshments, or smoking peacefully in the cool shade of leafy trees.

In many places there are good turf courts, but at others, where grass will not grow sufficiently well to be of any practical value, recourse is had to either cement or cinders.

Chinese lads in neat cotton uniforms are always in attendance to field the balls, which they do remarkably well, thereby adding greatly to one's enjoyment of the game.

Golf has of late years come greatly into prominence, a frequent place for the links being on the recreation ground enclosed by the race-track, for which reason it is generally the case that they are too flat to afford much variety of play, although near to Macao there are some very rough links which, from the natural advantages and lovely scenery, could be made almost ideal.

Our club there consisted of six members when at its zenith, and occasionally two in times of dearth. We had three miles to bicycle out, and part of the way over a fearful stone road through nauseous burial-grounds, but once there, a round or two in cool, fresh air, amongst the hills and pines, overlooking both sea and river, amply repaid one for the toilsome journey.

Of rowing there is very little, except at Shanghai and Hongkong, where there are large and flourishing clubs.

Hongkong being on the sea it is not practicable to use light ships, which, of course, is a great drawback.

At Shanghai there is the harbour and also a small creek about the size of the Cam, both of which afford ample facilities. The club has two excellent boathouses and plenty of boats, and is composed of the finest material possible, all the best men in Shanghai, as is ever the case elsewhere, going in for rowing at one time or another; but the rowing is not first-class, and unless things have greatly changed since I was an active member, a crew capable of sitting a light cedar ship could not be mustered, all the racing being done in clinker boats.

The reason for this lack of watermanship is partly due to the difficulty in coaching otherwise than from the stern of a boat, there being no towing path on which the coach can ride or run alongside his men, as is done at Oxford or Cambridge, while the hire of launches is too expensive. Also, part of the reason is due to beginners being seldom taken out and coached in tubs by expert senior men who have had the benefit of a professional or scientific training, but are put into a bad four and left to develop themselves as best they may. It would well repay the club to have a path made alongside the creek and to get a professional out from home for a year or two to initiate a high-class style, after which the traditions, once firmly established, would pass down naturally to succeeding generations of oarsmen.

The coxing is on a par with the rowing. I have seen a length lost at a corner, the rate of striking reduced by ten a minute and the crew badly pulled to pieces, through the rudder being hard on when the oars were in the water.

After all, skill in rowing is but a question of degree and of no vital importance in a place so isolated from other rowing centres as is Shanghai, while the club is certainly one of the best to get into on arriving there, especially for youths, as plenty of good, open-air exercise can thus be obtained in the society of strong, healthy-minded men.

If hills or mountains be within easy distance bungalows are there built, to which most ladies and children retire for the hot weather, the men snatching hasty visits when business allows them to leave the settlement. At one place down south such bungalows are built on a tiny island four or five miles out at sea, and there it is never very hot, while in the evenings it is delightful to bathe, stroll along the sands, or sit with the pilot on watch up by the old ruined fort, where you can see rays from the lighthouses flashing far, far across the waves, watch the lights of steamers as they pass beneath and listen to the cadenced throbbing of their screws. For those residing in Central China a sanatorium has lately sprung up near Kiukiang, at Kuling, a valley some 4,000 feet above sea-level in the Lushan mountains, which overlook the Yangtse on one side and the Poyang lake on the other. This valley was unknown to Europeans a few years ago, but has now the appearance of a country town, there being probably a hundred and fifty well-appointed bungalows strongly built of stone quarried on the spot, a church, shops, laundry and a network of roads and paths.

When feeling run down after a long spell of intense heat in the plains, a trip to this resort is most refreshing, for there it is always cool enough to wear light tweeds during the day and to sleep under a blanket at night. The mountain rambles are lovely, be it over the lofty peaks, through the trees and scrub in the valleys or along the bed of a stream, where frequent pools of running, crystal water afford good bathing or a little fishing for those addicted to the gentle art.

Never shall I forget one glorious day when, accompanying two friends, we crossed to a far side of the range and looked down on the Poyang lake. The view was magnificent, and on our return journey the setting sun flashed every imaginable hue on the mists rolling close above our heads, on the landscape changing as we moved, on mountain crags and on the lake, unfolding at each turn dissolving scenes of surpassing loveliness.

On arrival at Kiukiang by steamer you hire a chair with four bearers for the ten or twelve miles' journey up the mountains, with additional coolies to carry your luggage. For half the distance you follow ordinary country roads, but during the last few miles the path, though well constructed, is very steep in some places, while in others it overhangs yawning valleys, where you instinctively grip the sides of your chair and fervently hope the bearers will not trip.

In the north, Chefoo, Wei-hai-wei and Pei-tai-ho attract a goodly number of visitors to the seaside during summer months, while others desiring greater change sail to earth's fairyland, Japan, or even make the voyage to Canada and back.

We dance whenever and wherever we can. The houses being generally large, with fine rooms often but lightly furnished on account of the summer heat or our own nomadic habits, and servants being both plentiful and willing, the giving of a dance presents no great difficulties.

It is a common thing at a dinner-party of twelve or fourteen to have the drawing-room cleared during dinner, so that with the help of a few more friends who come in afterwards, the evening's entertainment can be pleasantly varied with a few dances.

I was once at a small port where for a long time there had been only one lady, who was naturally regarded as the belle of the place. Presently a rival appeared, and with her two pretty, unmarried sisters; whereon my messmates and I forthwith gave an impromptu dance.

We cleared our dining-room for the occasion, but found the carpet to be so old and so tightly nailed down that it would not bear removing, and we decided to dance on it.

No sooner, however, had we commenced to the strains of an accordion, not having a piano, than the floor, which was laid on round joists over the entrance hall, began to vibrate so violently that glasses on the sideboard were smashed and ornaments fell from the walls, while dust from the carpet, which evidently had not been beaten for years, rose in such clouds that, coupled with the heat of a stifling night, we were literally choked off and obliged to take refuge in the garden. Fortunately it was a beautiful night and full moon, so we diverted our dance to a game of hide-and-seek, and a merrier evening I have seldom spent.

The annual out-port subscription ball keeps everyone in a ferment for weeks. Owing to the cosmopolitan nature of the community due care must be taken that the various nationalities are represented on the committee, to avoid giving offence.

Then the committee has to decide, amongst other things, who are to be invited and who not, and it invariably happens that some are for including all, irrespective of station, while others desire to draw the line after what they consider to be the 閘 ite. In either case there is bound to be a certain amount of friction, which at times rises to a very heated pitch.

One of the leading ladies superintends the decoration of the ballroom, another is responsible for the supper, while another sees that the floor is properly waxed and arranges for the piano, as the music is provided by leading amateurs, there being no band.

After endless discussion and elaborate preparation the important night arrives, when the guests assemble, frequently with strained feelings but with a fixed determination to enjoy the passing hour.

Men are largely in the majority, so that ladies of all ages, ranging say from fourteen to forty, are requested as a favour to dance, and are assured beforehand of a full programme.

Those men who cannot get partners, or do not care to dance, spend the evening between cards and occasional visits to the ballroom to watch.

The supper is always very good and not hurried through with that undue haste so noticeable at home. The assembly, being considerably leavened with people who are, to say the least, well out of their teens, makes itself comfortable for an hour or more, doing ample justice to the delicacies provided; indeed, after the ladies have all departed, bachelors and wayward husbands usually return to the attack once, and even twice, so that it is not uncommon to hear an incoherent "For he's a jolly good fellow" from a belated band of revellers returning home shortly before daylight.

At Peking, Hongkong and Shanghai dances and balls are very frequent and carried out on a scale comparable with that of similar festivities at home.

The club is always a popular institution, where the male element of the community, frequently representing many nationalities, gathers for a game of billiards and a chat, and where the home and local papers, together with a fair number of books and magazines, are to be found. One evening during the tea season, just before dinner, I counted at one time fourteen nationalities in the bar of the Hankow Club.

I like those friendly gatherings at the round table, when sport and other topics of our limited world are discussed, and when one generally manages to give or to receive an invitation to pot-luck, with a rubber or a gentle poker flutter to follow.

There, too, is sometimes an American bowling alley, where on cold nights, or hot, for the matter of that, we roll huge wooden balls down a raised track for twenty yards, to scatter nine pins at the bottom. There are two parallel tracks and we make up two bowling parties of three or four aside, the losers to pay for the game and provide refreshments all round.

China is so enormous in extent that it embraces almost every variety of climate, though, speaking generally, the summer is everywhere very warm, while the winter, from being almost of arctic severity in the northern provinces, where the sea is frozen and all navigation stopped for six weeks or two months, gradually becomes milder in lower latitudes, until snow and frost are seldom experienced, and finally never seen in the sub-tropical region of the extreme south. Many years ago snow fell at Canton and the astonished natives are said to have collected it in bottles to keep, believing that it was a kind of cotton.

In the Yangtse valley during July, August and September, the heat at times is well-nigh intolerable both by day and night. You arise in the morning played out after a comfortless night under a punkah, which, hung over your bed in the limited space of a mosquito house, is pulled with a rope passing through the wall by a coolie stationed on the verandah outside. With the thermometer standing at ninety degrees in your bedroom you frame the mental query "Can I last through the day?" as you crawl on to the verandah in pyjamas wet through with perspiration, to watch the sun rise, hoping, but in vain, for a breath of air. The insects buzz, a scorched smell pervades everywhere, the birds hop listlessly about, gasping with wide-open bills, the fans of coolies who have been sleeping on the grass, beat with hollow flap, the sun rises like a furnace, and you must retreat again to the shadow of your room to avoid sunstroke.

As the day advances the temperature creeps up until it is over a hundred and you feel your eyes dry and heavy in their sockets, with a throbbing in your ears, when for full-blooded people of any age it becomes highly dangerous, death by heat apoplexy being painfully common.

In the evening, after dinner, long chairs are taken out on the bund and many assemble there in silence, betrayed only in the darkness by a continual popping of corks and glowing cigar-tips, to catch what little air there may chance to be, and to watch the lightning in hopes that the oft-threatened storm will burst and break the heat.

I remember at Kiukiang the daily temperature rising to over a hundred degrees in the shade for nearly three weeks at a stretch, culminating in one hundred and seven, when a break came which, at any rate, saved my life and practically ended the summer.

Many a time, when too hot for sleep, have I played whist till three o'clock in the morning. Selecting the corner of an upstairs verandah where there might be some possibility of a faint draught, and having cigars, whisky and iced soda well within reach, we would take off our white jackets for greater coolness and sit perspiring in singlets round the table between guttering candles, when with bare heads and naked arms we must have had the appearance of desperate gamblers, though only playing the regulation twenty-five cent points with longs and shorts and a dollar on the rub, so that the damage could not be very extensive.

The winter in this locality is very much on a par with that in England, only shorter, there being generally some frost with a good deal of snow and occasionally enough ice for skating.

Dinner-parties are very numerous, being the chief method of entertainment. The menu is, as a rule, excellent, and the import duty being almost nominal, wine is both plentiful and good.

After a few mental twinges endured by leading personages consequent on somewhat exaggerated ideas of precedence, the company is seated, and a good dinner, aided by a lively flow of chit-chat, makes the evening speed pleasantly and well.

But, you will ask, what besides amusing themselves have these Anglo-Chinese to do? British steamers swarm throughout the China seas and up the Yangtse for a thousand miles to Ichang, and it is in controlling the working of these vessels, in importing and selling manufactured goods and opium, in buying and exporting tea, silk and other products of the country, as well as in filling positions in Government services or any professional calling that agents, merchants, officials and the professional classes find employment, so that if in exile we surround ourselves with such luxuries and enjoyments as are reserved for the wealthy at home it is because they are ready to hand at but little cost, and that they serve in a degree to compensate us for the sweet pleasures of home-life which are forfeited by those who leave Old England to push their ways in distant lands.

CHAPTER II

SERVANTS AND TRADESMEN

On your first arrival at an out-port, and as you are crossing the pontoon which leads from the steamer to the bund, a most beaming celestial meets you and presents an open letter, which runs something like this:--

"I hereby certify that the bearer, Lao San, was my boy for eight months, and I found him honest and willing. TOM JONES."

The celestial smirks and jabbers something in pidgin English, which not being able to understand you answer with a grunt and pass on.

The celestial says, "All right, savez, can do," and vanishes.

Reaching your quarters, you find two or three more beaming natives, also armed with letters of recommendation, probably borrowed for the occasion, and who severally inform you "My b'long welly good boy."

These letters of recommendation become kinds of heirlooms, and as foreigners seldom know the correct names of their Chinese servants, they are, for a consideration, handed about from one to the other when seeking employment.

You must have a boy anyhow, and are just beginning to inspect the candidates when a friend suddenly turns up.

"I'm awfully sorry, old man, I couldn't manage to come and meet you on board, but the steamer arrived earlier than was expected, so I came straight on here, and knowing you would require a boy, brought one along who wants a job. I don't know anything about him, but he says he's all right, and they are mostly pretty much alike. Anyhow, you might give him a trial, and if he doesn't suit, just kick him out."

Before you can reply the door is thrown violently open, and your luggage, which you had left for the time being in your cabin on the steamer, is brought in on bamboo poles by half-a-dozen coolies and dumped on the floor, the beaming celestial who met you on the pontoon following close behind, carrying your collection of sun hats, umbrellas and sticks. He immediately pays the coolies, unstraps rugs and trunks, and commences to arrange the room.

Your friend says, "Oh, I didn't know you had brought your own boy," and goes on to talk of other things.

You feel rather pleased at all the luggage having turned up without any effort on your part, pleased at being freed from the importunities of out-of-work boys, and dumbly acquiesce, so that Lao San remains until you have the time or inclination to engage a really good boy; but as you seldom have the time, and never the inclination, he is already pretty firmly established.

In the course of the day he introduces a cook as well as two or three coolies that you do not want but must have, and explains that all these men are of exceptionally good character, and that he "can secure b'long all ploper." You submit, of course, and so your household is arranged by the boy without you really having had a word to say. A day or two later you suddenly remember that nothing has been said on the subject of wages.

You ring up the boy, and after a short discussion it is arranged that he is to receive eight dollars a month, the cook ten, and the coolies six and five. Everything is arranged with the boy, the other servants not appearing on the scene at all, and so it is that, having obtained situations for his friends, they are by "olo custom" obliged to pay him a squeeze on their salaries, the cook probably two dollars a month and the coolies one each. Without your consent or knowledge the cook introduces a young friend of his into the kitchen to be known as the "second cook," or simply "No 2." His position corresponds to that of the scullery-maid, washing up pots and pans, lighting the fire and running errands, in return for which he receives very little, if any, pay, but learns the art of cooking. Your house is now in going order, and at first things really work very well under the boy's supervision.

A few weeks later it suddenly dawns on you that expenses are mounting up in rather an unaccountable way, and you look into matters.

Nothing very serious comes to light, and any doubtful little points are most clearly explained away by the boy. However, it is not long before you again begin to feel uneasy and insist on knowing details of the various small accounts which are monthly presented to you by each individual on the premises.

You are being squeezed by all!

The boy charges for a number of small items such as lampwick, matches, soap, candles, etc., that you have never had, or in half the quantities stated. Also, on things which you have had, a large percentage over cost price is levied. All the native tradesmen are in league with your servants, and while you know that you are being swindled it would be quite impossible to prove it, for should a shopkeeper or butcher tell you what his prices really were he would lose much of his business, as servants in foreign employ would, in time, by some means or other, take the custom elsewhere.

You are the means whereby a large but limited circle of Chinese manage to live and oftentimes save money. All members of the circle regard you as their prey, and tacitly combining to play into each other's hands they fleece you with impunity, it being extremely difficult, if not impossible, to get one Chinaman to expose or bear witness against another, especially if it be with the object of benefiting the foreigner.

The best way for a bachelor to run his house is to set aside a certain sum which he knows should be sufficient for monthly expenditure. If he can keep his expenses below this figure so much the better. If he cannot, and they exceed it, he should cut down the various accounts until a sufficient reduction has been reached. It is useless trying to argue the case, he would always come off worsted.

I heard of one bachelor who had been drawing a salary of six hundred dollars a month, but he kept up such style that he could only just cover expenses. After a time his business partly failed, so he sent for the boy and explained he could only spend four hundred dollars. The domestic pulled a long face, but the style of living was not altered in the least.

Again bad times came and expenditure had to be further reduced to three hundred dollars a month. The bachelor informed his servant that he had better get another situation as he feared it would be difficult for him to come down from six hundred dollars to three hundred, and that it would be wiser to start a fresh establishment more in accordance with his reduced circumstances.

After reflection the boy decided to struggle on, and this he did with such success that the style of living was exactly the same as it had ever been.

The word "boy" bears no reference whatever to the individual's age, which may be anything between sixteen and sixty. It is merely a term applied by foreigners to their personal attendants.

The duties of the boy are those of the ordinary housekeeper in England, with several additions.

He looks after the other servants and is generally responsible for their good behaviour. He pays all wages and the accounts of the local tradespeople, on which, of course, he levies a recognised squeeze. He waits at table, answers the bell, makes the beds and brushes his master's clothes, in fact, makes himself generally useful.

As a rule, he accompanies his master to all dinner-parties to assist in waiting. Also, it is a common and recognised practice for the boy of a house where a big dinner or a dance is being held to borrow requisites from the boy of another house, and often without reference to the owner, so that when dining out you not infrequently drink from your own glasses, use your own knives and forks, see your own lamp on the dinner-table and are waited on by your own servant.

A Scotchman who had recently married brought from London a goodly supply of fine glassware for the new home. At one of the dinner-parties given in honour of himself and bride, after replying to the toast of the evening he proposed the health of his host and requested the company to drink it with Highland honours by placing one foot on the table and one on the chair. Bumpers having been tossed off he added that it would not be fitting for glasses consecrated by such distinguished service to thereafter descend to ordinary usage, and suiting the action to the word, flung the tumbler over his shoulder, so that it was shivered to atoms against the wall, the other guests, numbering upwards of a dozen, following suit.

His boy's placid comment on the proceeding was, "Truly master b'long too muchee foolo, he no savez b'long he new glass."

They were indeed his own beautiful tumblers, borrowed for the occasion without his knowledge.

If anything is lost in the house, the boy, being answerable, is supposed to make the loss good, although he seldom does so. It may be imagined that his post is no sinecure with an exacting master, but it is lucrative and one much sought after.

The custom of servants mutually guaranteeing each other's good conduct is a great safeguard, for in the case of theft or other misdemeanour by one of them, all the others are responsible and severe measures may be taken against them with the view of discovering the culprit, so that in reality while subject to numberless irritating, petty pilferings, against which there is no guarding and for which it is impossible to obtain redress, it rarely happens that any serious offence is committed.

Amongst themselves the Chinese carry this principle of responsibility to such great lengths that if after committing a crime the culprit flees from justice, the officials can, and often do, arrest his father, mother, wife and whole family, and both imprison and persecute them until the fugitive gives himself up; and such is the strength of the family tie that this arbitrary method is seldom known to fail.

The cook is, next to the boy, the most important of the other servants, and as a rule is fairly efficient, some indeed being excellent, although great care must be taken to guard against their natural love of filthiness. A kitchen into which the master or mistress of the house does not go once or twice every day should never be visited at all if one wishes to enjoy one's meals.

This is also a lucrative post, for besides wages and a heavy squeeze on every article brought into the kitchen, the remains of each meal, whether half a chicken, half a leg of mutton, or both, are regarded by the cook as his perquisite and carried off for sale to native restaurants, unless special orders have been given to the contrary. A reason for this is that in hot climates food, if not eaten at once, quickly becomes worse than useless. Also, owing to the cheapness of meat, eggs, vegetables, etc., it is by no means the serious loss that it would be at home, and so the householder is generally not sorry that the remains of each meal should disappear and thus get fresh food at every repast.

The cooking in foreign houses is entirely European, the Chinese cuisine being of a very different and truly wonderful kind, although excellent in quality. Western ladies have often taken great pains to train their cooks to a high standard of proficiency, a well-served dinner in China not uncommonly far surpassing in excellence the corresponding meal at home. Of course, the reverse is frequently the case, still, it serves to show that the Chinese have a great faculty for the culinary art.

In England a dinner-party must be arranged some days beforehand in order that the necessary preparations may be made, and it is practically impossible to suddenly announce at tea-time that there will be eight people to dinner instead of two.

This matter is certainly managed better in China.

Oftentimes on returning from office at five o'clock I have sent for the cook and said, "To-night eight piecee man catchee dinner. Can do, no can do?" and the reply has invariably been a laconic "Can do."

At once there would be great bustling but no confusion, and it has always seemed to me that these sudden demands on the kitchen staff, instead of evoking complaints and sullen looks, are regarded rather as a source of pleasurable excitement. "No 2" hurries off to market and quickly returns with fish, chops, chickens, eggs and fruit. Meanwhile, the cook dashes another pint or two of water into the soup and gets a jam pudding well under way.

On returning from the club at seven o'clock you find that the boy has tastefully laid the table and decorated it with leaves and flowers. After seeing to the wine and cigars you go up to dress, and on receiving your guests at half-past seven the dinner is ready.

I remember with feelings of pleasure the following incident which occurred at Chinkiang.

For some days I had been engaged to dine with friends living in the next house, and was actually on my way there, when an old acquaintance, who had just arrived by the steamer from Shanghai, met me in the garden and wanted particularly to see me with regard to some private affair. As the steamer would be leaving again in two hours and my friend was obliged to continue his voyage to Hankow, I had no other means of meeting his wishes than by forfeiting my engagement. This I did in a hastily-written chit, making the best excuses I could, and then sent for the cook. On his appearance I informed him that I wanted dinner for two--chop chop! Without moving a muscle he answered, "Can do." Thinking to hurry up matters a little I went to the kitchen, but found it in darkness and without any fire. The servants meanwhile had all disappeared, and I returned to my friend with the information that we must possess our souls in patience, so we settled ourselves on the verandah for a serious talk, but hardly had we done so than the boy announced dinner.

Following him in considerable amazement I found that, the night being warm, he had laid a small table on the lawn and that the soup was already served. It was delicious, as were also the samli, the woodcock, the lamb cutlets and the ice-cream. Things having taken so happy a turn, I uncorked a bottle of champagne and we had a banquet fit for a king.

My friend complimented me on the prowess of the cook, and we smoked our cigars and chatted over the coffee until the steamer's whistle announced that, cargo being finished, she was ready to start. After seeing him off I joined the party next door in order to offer apologies and explanations to the hostess, who freely forgave me, though her husband lamented that I had missed the samli, the woodcock and the lamb, which were the first of the season.

I discreetly held my peace, but inquiries next day confirmed my suspicions that prime helpings from each course of my neighbour's dinner had been carried off by my cook.

Immediately under the boy for indoor work is the "house-coolie," whose business it is to swab floors, polish grates, light fires, trim lamps, clean knives and boots and make himself generally useful about the house. Oftentimes he is unable to speak any English, wears a short coat in contradistinction to the boy's long one, and while ranking below the boy is considerably above the other coolies as having better pay, pleasanter work and holding a position of trust.

At the chief entrance to most residences is a gatehouse, tenanted during the day by an old man who serves as gatekeeper, and who is responsible for keeping bad characters off the premises as well as for not allowing anything to be taken away. At sunset he goes home, being relieved by the night-watchman, who remains on duty till sunrise. He also is responsible for the general safety, and is not supposed to sleep during the night, but to be on guard. Every two hours, that is, at each of the five watches into which the night is divided, he should make a round of the outbuildings to satisfy himself that all's well. This he does not do quietly, but to the beating of a bamboo rattle, so that thieves may know he is on the lookout and run away. Sometimes, in order to keep up his courage, I have even heard him shout "I see you," "I know who you are," "I'm coming," "Who's afraid?" etc.

Ridiculous as this may appear to English burglars it is yet very effective, though for a very curious reason.

China is the country of guilds, every trade being in the hands of a certain section of the population, who combine against all intruders. There is a guild of water-carriers, a guild of fortune-tellers, a guild of pipe-makers, and even a guild of thieves. This last is a recognised body, and is treated with by all householders, until it has become a kind of insurance agency against theft. All gatekeepers and night-watchmen pay a small monthly fee to this guild in order that no thieving may take place on the premises over which they have control, and the system works well, for not only is anything rarely stolen, but if, occasionally, something does go it is almost certain to have been taken by a free lance, who would be promptly done to death should he fall into the clutches of the guild thieves.

A friend of mine who employs many hundreds of coolies pays a regular monthly salary to the head of the thieves in that district. This man comes to the office on pay-days like other employ 閟 to draw his wages. If, however, anything has been missed from the factory during the month the value of it is deducted from his salary until the article is restored, which is invariably done.

I have heard of a case where a reforming spirit determined not to submit to such an iniquitous tax. The gatekeeper and night-watchman immediately resigned and could not be replaced, while by the end of the month most of his portable belongings had been surreptitiously removed. Thoroughly cowed, he recalled the two servants and instructed them to pay the tax, whereupon the stolen articles promptly reappeared and security was again restored.

Largely owing to the influence of Buddhism, cattle are regarded by the Chinese solely as beasts of burden, it being seldom that any are slaughtered for food; and although many natives will eat beef when it comes conveniently to hand, still, there is a strong prejudice against it. This prejudice extends both to milk and butter, neither of which is a common article of celestial food. From this it may be easily imagined that Europeans are often put to considerable inconvenience in securing an adequate supply of these daily necessaries. Good milk is especially hard to get. So long as it is white the native dairyman considers that his obligations to customers are discharged, while the more water he can add, the better it is for his own pocket. At Hankow the supply was so adulterated that a friend of mine actually found a small live fish in his morning cupful. With a view to exposing fraud I purchased a lactometer and found the usual proportions of milk and water to be half and half.

This was too much, so calling the dairyman to the house I abused him roundly and threatened that if he did not send pure milk in future I would ask the consul to punish him severely. He vowed and declared that the lactometer "no talkee true," and that no water whatever had been added to the milk, adding, that if I did not believe him he would bring a cow to the kitchen door and I could see it milked myself.

This seemed satisfactory, so I got up early next morning, and after shivering in my dressing-gown during the milking, carried off the pail in triumph, fully convinced that I should now be able to enjoy the pure article. Vain delusion! On testing it there was still a large percentage of water, and the dairyman, beaming with justified satisfaction, ambled off, leading his cow.

Feeling sure that the lactometer must be at fault, I consulted my friend the doctor, who examined and found it quite correct.

How to reconcile these discrepancies seemed an insoluble problem.

After pondering over the matter for several days, I determined on milking the cow myself, this being an accomplishment of my boyhood. To the celestial's amazement I did so and instantly tested the proceeds. Pure milk!

I seized the dairyman with a hazy idea of making an end of him, when, lo and behold, there slipped from his capacious sleeve a piece of thick bamboo containing about two pints of water. From the lower part of this wooden bottle projected another piece of bamboo about the thickness of a cigar, which served as a tube.

The swindle was now discovered, and the culprit, after the first shock to his feelings had abated, showed me, with evident if subdued satisfaction, how the ingenious device worked.

Concealing the bottle and letting the sleeve fall well down over his wrist, he held the bamboo tube and a cow's teat in one hand, and so, the moment one's eyes were averted, he was able to turn on the tap and let water flow into the pail together with the milk.

I now had the upper hand and promised to refrain from taking steps against him if he would in future furnish me with a pure supply. This he cheerfully agreed to do, and for a time I fared sumptuously, but it was not long ere my boy informed me that, the cows having run dry, the dairyman had returned to his home in the country.

Prior to the Manchu conquest of China two hundred and fifty years ago, men allowed the hair to grow long and then rolled it up in a tuft on the top of the head.

The Manchus, however, introduced the custom of partly shaving the scalp and braiding the back hair into a pig-tail, any man not conforming to this rule being considered a rebel, and as such liable to summary decapitation. This visible token of loyalty to the present dynasty is therefore universal, and obtains from the cradle to the grave, it being a matter of considerable importance to all who value a whole skin, and "Olo custom" being an extremely strong motif, it would now be well-nigh impossible to abolish this badge of servitude, even were the enforcement of it abandoned. In addition to this national obligation it is the custom for men to clean shave until they become grandfathers, when a moustache is cultivated, and later on sometimes a beard, though these hirsute appendages are of a lean and meagre kind.

As you may readily imagine, the amount of tonsorial operations indulged in by so dense a population call for an unlimited number of shavers and braiders of hair, albeit it is considered an employment of the lowest grade; but although the number of barbers is legion there are none who know how to cut hair until taught to do so by Europeans, so that in out-of-the-way places it is often very difficult to get the operation performed. On several occasions I have been obliged to rely on my mafoo, who with horse-clippers and iron scissors proved to be effective if somewhat unartistic.

Of course, a Chinaman will soon learn, and at treaty-ports barbers are a convenient luxury, for at the cost of a few dollars a month one will come to your bedroom every morning at a stated time to perform the daily shave, as well as cut the hair when required. Oftentimes I have been still asleep when, leaving his shoes outside the door and creeping in noiselessly with bare feet, he has adjusted the towel, lathered and shaved me in bed without my having had more than a dim consciousness of what was going on.

Tailors are cheap and plentiful. A West-end cut is not achieved, but for flannels, light tweeds and all such clothes as are worn in the tropics, they are very passable.

"Boy."

"Sai."

"Talkee that tailor-man four o'clock come. Wantchee new clothes."

At four o'clock the tailor is there with a bundle of patterns from which you select a thin serge and a white flannel, and order a suit of each. On asking the price you are informed that the serge "b'long welly cheap" at fourteen dollars and the flannel at twelve.

Your surprise and indignation are great at the exorbitant figures, and after a good deal of haggling, eleven dollars and ten respectively are agreed upon, the clothes to be finished in two days.

"Can do."

Out comes the tape and he measures you all over, taking mental notes but writing nothing down, the Chinese having marvellous memories.

Next morning he appears with the garments loosely stitched together to try on, draws a chalk line here, puts in a pin there and hurries off.

The following day you discover both suits neatly folded up on your bed, and on inspection find them to be of good and comfortable fit.

Another plan is, after selecting the material, to hand the tailor an old suit with instructions to make the new one a counterpart of it, which, as a rule, he will do to perfection. In fact, he has been known to let a couple of patches into the seat of the new trousers in order to make them correspond exactly with the pattern.

CHAPTER III

SHOOTING

To anyone who is fond of shooting, certain parts of China offer a veritable paradise. When I say shooting I do not mean the kind of sport to which one is accustomed at home, where to trespass a few yards on the grounds of another man will probably result in legal proceedings, where keepers flourish and wax fat on contributions levied on the friends of mine host, where hand-raised game is driven into the jaws of death, and where the sportsman's friend and delight, his dog, is practically banished. No, I mean where one can look on the whole empire of China and say, "Here is my ground, here I can take my gun and my dogs and go just wherever, and do whatever, I please, without let or hindrance; shoot what I will, stay as long as I like without asking anyone's leave, and where keepers and game licences are unknown."

Throughout China, pheasants, deer, quail, wildfowl and snipe abound, but woodcock, partridges and hares are less numerous and less evenly distributed. Bustards, plover and many other migratory birds appear only in winter, while for hunters of big game, tigers, leopards, horned deer and wild boar are found in certain localities.

Northern China offers the best opportunities, and while from Mongolia to Ningpo game is plentiful enough, the mighty River Yangtse is par excellence the sportsman's elysium. Of course, one must have good dogs and know the country, or go with someone who does, otherwise the most ardent spirit would soon be cooled to freezing point and disgust instead of delight would be the result of his endeavours. Along the banks of this noble river, from the sea for hundreds of miles into the interior, I have enjoyed as good sport as lies within reach of only the very rich in western countries.

The Chinese are not often sportsmen, and away from foreign influence but rarely molest wild animals of any kind.

Owing, however, to the increasing European colony at Shanghai and the numerous mail steamers which daily arrive there, a profitable market for game has sprung up during the past few years, to supply which there are now a number of native gunners who, as a means of livelihood, scour the country with foreign breech-loaders in search of pheasants, wildfowl, etc., so that, being capital shots, within a considerable distance of this port the shooting is not so good as formerly, although in all other parts of the Empire it still remains practically untouched until the advent of Europeans.

That there are not more aboriginal sportsmen is partly due to a law which forbids the people to possess firearms, though this law has not been rigidly enforced, and partly due to the primitive construction and consequent unreliability of the few native fowling-pieces which do exist.

Well away from beaten tracks I have occasionally met local sports carrying guns together with slow-matches of smouldering brown paper. They are remarkable weapons, with single iron barrels some four feet and a half long, about twenty bore and without stocks, but having pistol handles. There are no locks or springs, the hammer and trigger being in one piece, working through the handle on a rivet. The hammers have slits in them as if to hold flints, but which really are intended for the slow-match. Sometimes these men had good bags of snipe, but only once have I seen such a gun fired, which was at a pigeon sitting about fifteen yards high in a tree. The gunner blew his slow-match into a glow and pressed it into the slit in the hammer, placed the pistol handle to his hip and pulled the trigger, which brought the hammer slowly forward until the slow-match rested on the powder in the pan, when the gun went off and the pigeon fell dead. Whether birds are shot on the wing with these guns I cannot say, but remembering that a hundred and fifty years ago it was accounted an extraordinary thing to attempt flying shots even in this country, I should think probably not.

Old muzzle-loading rifles of European make, striking either flints or percussion caps, are also in occasional use as shot-guns, in preference to native weapons.

The shot are always of iron, which is far cheaper than lead, and extremely liable to cause great injury to the teeth, while the powder is very poor, burning slowly with much smoke and smell. No cut wads are used, but pieces of paper, rammed home with a rod, which instead of being carried attached to the gun is held in the hand together with the slow-match.

These same sports catch snipe in long, light nets which they carry stretched out horizontally some two feet above the grass, so that a bird on rising as it passes overhead, flies into it and is at once secured. Snares of wire and string, ingenious traps of bamboo which impale the birds on wooden spikes, and wicker traps closely resembling the straw plaiting on bottles of olive oil, I have seen set for snipe and quail in various places.

I once travelled from Shanghai to Nanking with an aged French Jesuit priest and a Chinese official then returning from the Black Dragon or Amour river. The former told me that, shortly after the Taiping rebellion, pheasants were so numerous and tame in the devastated fields around Nanking that natives speared them in the grass; while the official said that in the almost deserted Black Dragon river district these birds were so little afraid of man that on his approach they would conceal only their heads in the grass, when it was possible to capture them by the tail with the hand. Although personally unable to guarantee either of these accounts, still, judging from the manner in which they were narrated, I am inclined to believe both.

The first essential for shooting-trips up the Yangtse is a good house-boat or light draft yacht of from ten to fifteen tons, into which you pack every requisite, and which is in reality your floating shooting-box for the time being. You have only to choose your field of operations, sail there, and enjoy yourself to your heart's content in luxury, fine bracing air, grand scenery and jovial company. What can one wish for more!

Having decided on a trip you tell your boy in the morning that you will leave that afternoon for so many days, and at the appointed time step on board to find everything in readiness--guns, dogs, provisions, and a good fire in the saloon. You give the lowdah his orders, and in less than a minute are under way. All bother is at an end and you make yourself comfortable, have afternoon tea, read, smoke, dine, chat with your friend over the fire, and after spending the evening as comfortably as if in your own house, retire to rest, awaking next morning to find yourself on the scene of action and very possibly to hear the pheasants crow while still in bed. A good beefsteak breakfast and you are ready for the fray. After your day's sport you come back to a hot bath and the comfort of a cosy cabin. Should you desire to try fresh ground on the morrow, the lowdah will get the boat there, either by sailing or tracking during the night, while you are enjoying your well-earned sleep.

Pheasants afford the principal sport and are identical with the white-ringed English birds, only, if any thing, bigger, stronger in flight and much more wily.

A hundred miles up the Yangtse and then along the Grand Canal, in districts that were overrun by Taiping rebels, fine sport with pointers may be had over what were formerly cultivated fields but are now still lying waste, with here and there the ruins of a village destroyed forty years ago, the inhabitants of which were either extirpated, dragged off in the rebel army or fled to other parts of the country. These abandoned fields, interspersed with ridges of low hills clad with young pines, are generally dry and covered with fine grass, in which the pheasants are fond of lying, and on a bright, frosty morning it is truly delightful to walk across such country with a couple of good pointers, watch your dogs work and bowl over the birds as they rise.

At other places higher up river the low hills are covered with acorn-bearing oak scrub, a favourite cover both for pheasants, which feed on the acorns, as well as deer. This scrub, although very trying to walk through, is not high enough to prevent pointers working freely, and many a good bag have I made there.

Along the banks of the lower Yangtse, and on numerous islands in the stream, are dense reeds, which, being flooded to a depth of several feet in summer, grow from fifteen to twenty feet high, as thick as a man's thumb, and almost as strong as bamboos. In these impenetrable thickets, left dry as the waters fall in autumn, the pheasants congregate in great numbers, but it is not till late winter, when the reeds have been mostly cut for fuel, that it is possible to get them out. About the end of December the reeds still uncut, stand in square, even patches, the sides of which tower up like the walls of a house. The best way is to select clumps of medium size, place a gun on either side to keep well in advance, and turn two or three dogs, spaniels for choice, in at one end. As these dogs hunt the reeds all the way down, the pheasants will creep to the very edges, watch their opportunity, and be off like cannon balls. Then is the time for a quick eye and steady hand, but as you have probably been running to keep up with the dogs, they are by no means the easy shots that one might imagine, and many a time the "dead certainty" has slipped gaily away.

Other denizens of these swamps are woodcock, snipe, deer, and occasionally racoons and wild cats, which follow the pheasants, so that a mixed bag is frequently the product of a successful day, when twenty-five head, including seven or eight brace of pheasants, would represent a fair average per gun. With the exception of spring snipe, enormous totals like those we gloat over in England are but rarely made. It is the absolute freedom which is so charming, the hard work, the bright atmosphere, the thick cover, and the excitement of following the dogs.

Wildfowl of every description swarm during the spring and autumn migrations, for after nesting on the Siberian steppes they go down to the Sunny South in winter. Swan, geese, mallard, teal and countless varieties of duck literally cover the waters of the Yangtse for miles at a stretch, and will hardly rise to avoid the river-steamers as they pass, although extremely shy of approaching small boats, while every little pond or creek affords the probability of a shot. Wildfowl-shooting, however, is not largely gone in for, why, I can hardly say, unless it is that they are so superabundant as to make them seem hardly worth the powder and shot, that the distances to go for them are too great and the work of stalking too cold and tiresome, or that other kinds of shooting are more attractive.

Woodcock are often found in bamboo groves from which it is generally hard to flush them, while the cover is so thick that it is impossible to shoot until they come out, though be it only for an instant, when, topping the bamboos, they alight again on the opposite side. I have spent nearly an hour in killing a brace which, although I saw perhaps twenty times, I had the greatest difficulty in getting a snap at. They also frequent pine woods and heather on the hills, and are identical in appearance with the woodcock found in England.

During a severe winter at Chinkiang, word was brought in by natives that some children had been carried off by "dog-headed tigers," which monsters, after making lengthy inquiries, we assumed to be wolves.

With a view to getting a shot at these brutes, a friend and I went out overnight to the community bungalow, a distance of seven miles, and in the morning ranged warily through the pines and over the snow-clad hills, seeking for traces of the man-eaters, being joined towards noon by the British Consul. Carrying my twelve-bore fowling-piece loaded with a bullet in the right barrel and a charge of big shot in the left, the latter being full-choke, I was passing along the side of a steep hill at the foot of which, and some fifty feet below me, lay a frozen stream, when my dog-coolie, pointing downwards, cried, "Look at the fish!"

Beneath the clear ice, of perhaps a quarter of an inch in thickness, a mass of fish was swimming with the current. Instinctively I fired the left barrel at them, and was greatly surprised to behold a jet of water, broken ice and fish shoot up two or three feet high from a hole made by the shot. The dog-coolie rushed down and filled his cap with our unexpected prey, which we subsequently found to number twenty-two, varying from about two to four ounces in weight each. Concussion from the blow on the ice had stunned many, but others were bleeding from shot wounds.

After a fruitless search for the "dog-headed tigers" we walked back to Chinkiang that evening.

The cold weather having brought wildfowl of all descriptions I was off betimes next morning to some islands in the Yangtse, a few miles down river. An hour's sailing with wind and stream brought me to the desired spot, where I landed on the sandy beach, when my dog, glad to escape from confinement on board, ran to the top of a high dyke, or wall for preventing floods, some hundred yards distant, and put up hundreds of wild geese which had been preening themselves in the sun on the other side, where they had also found shelter from the cutting wind. The mighty roar of wings was the first intimation I had of their presence, and as they were well out of range, my dog came in for a reminder that his place for the time being was close to heel. Had they not been thus scared away I could have walked unobserved to within five yards of them.

Following the beach a little above high-water mark, I presently came to several small ponds surrounded with willows, out of the first of which some teal rose in a close bunch, when firing into the brown I knocked them all down except one, and that I accounted for with the other barrel. Falling into the pond, some that were winged gave a good deal of trouble by diving, but eventually they were all secured, being eight in number. Several ducks were scared away by my shots, but I here added half-a-dozen snipe to the bag.

Coming to some wide ditches choked with reeds and willows my dog put out pheasant after pheasant, but as they generally got up on the opposite side, where there was no gun, I only managed to secure seven, besides two woodcock.

While eating my lunch of sandwiches under the lee of a reedstack, I observed that numerous flights of wildfowl on passing from one branch of the river to another crossed a low, marshy corner of the island, so that presently I made my way there and crouched down amongst the rushes behind a dyke, having a small lagoon immediately at my back. Mallard, widgeon and many other kinds of fowl came over in such quick succession that for two hours I was kept fully occupied, and it was highly gratifying to hear a heavy splash in the lagoon after each successful shot.

As soon as the light began to fail I ceased firing and retrieved my birds, which numbered twenty-seven, including several varieties of fish ducks with serrated bills and, as I have subsequently learnt although then mistaking them for large divers, three goosanders. On my way back to the house-boat I surprised and shot a goose which was feeding close under the river bank, so that my total bag consisted of fifty-one head, and I always look back on that day as one of the most enjoyable I have ever spent.

The snipe-shooting cannot be surpassed anywhere in the world. In spring, after spending the winter in rich southern climes, these birds, following the returning warmth, slowly migrate to Siberia for nesting. They pass through Central China during May, arriving almost simultaneously, when for about three weeks one can have superb sport, and then they depart as suddenly as they came. One day they will swarm, and the next hardly a bird is to be seen.

Snipe-shooting at home one always associates with long boots, cold water, mud and marshes. Spring snipe-shooting in China is of a totally different kind.

Imagine a bright, warm day, with the sun almost too powerful, dry meadows with fresh, green grass, and clover about six inches high, fields of wheat and barley in ear and beans in flower, all Nature at her best. You take your gun with a plentiful supply of cartridges, a coolie to carry bottled beer and sandwiches and to pick up the birds, and sally forth into the meadows and fields, dressed in an ordinary light summer suit or flannels, terai hat and low shoes, with the bottoms of your trousers tucked into your socks to keep out the insects.

You have not gone far before one, two--half a dozen birds rise within easy range, and perhaps you make a right and left. What birds they are, too, fat as butter!--in fact, so fat and heavy that they often rip quite open merely from the force of falling to the ground. In this way you go on, firing until the gun becomes so hot that every now and then you must wait to let the barrels cool. My best bag for one day was forty-one and a half couples, but this has been doubled by sports who have shot to make a record.

Autumn snipe, or spring snipe returned, on passing from Siberia to winter in the south, are not usually in very good condition, owing probably to the nature of the country from which they come, and strangely enough they appear to be less numerous and do not arrive so simultaneously as the spring birds, though remaining longer, many staying on through the winter. These do not frequent the dry meadows and fields, but belong to the long boots, mud and marsh category.

I have never seen but one jack snipe, though the painted variety is fairly common.

In the neighbourhood of a creek seven miles below Hankow is to be had the best spring snipe-shooting that I know of. One bright May morning, in response to the invitation of an old friend, I joined him and two other guests aboard his house-boat and sailed down the Yangtse to this well-known spot. On landing I shouldered my bag, containing fifty cartridges, and told my coolie to bring a new box of a hundred in the game-bag.

The plan was to send the house-boat to a place three or four miles further down river, where, after shooting through the fields, the guns would meet for tiffin.

Just as the lowdah was casting off our host asked if he might put a few bottles of beer into my game-bag as it was a warm and thirsty morning; so, to make room, and thinking that the snipe had not yet fully arrived, in which case the spare cartridges would not be required, they were replaced on board. We had not, however, walked many yards along the river bank before it became apparent that there were any number of birds, and I already regretted having so few cartridges with me. After crossing the creek in a crazy sampan the party separated, each taking his own line of country. Presently a tremendous fusillade commenced from all the others, and as the snipe were rising around them continually and making for a large swamp to my left, I concealed myself in some millet, where, the birds coming before the wind directly over my head, I enjoyed for half an hour or so some excellent shooting and made a number of very sporting shots.

I now started for the swamp, but ere reaching it passed through some grass patches between fields of barley and beans. The birds here rose by the dozen, and standing on the same spot, without advancing a yard, I shot eight, which were all on the ground at one time. My gun became so hot that it was necessary to open it to let the barrels cool, while the cartridges were all gone in less than an hour, so that carrying my now useless weapon and boiling with rage, I had to start in pursuit of the house-boat, with the shots of the others ringing merrily all round, the snipe rising at almost every step, and the coolie laden with beer and dead birds lagging far behind.

I arrived on board simultaneously with a party of ladies, who, under the 鎔 is of my friend's wife, had come down by launch to join us at tiffin; at the conclusion of which long and sumptuous repast it was time to start back to Hankow rather than again attack the snipe. However, two of us landed with our guns and walked hurriedly across country towards a point about three miles up river, there to rejoin the party on the boat. Of course we kept them waiting, the sport was so good, but satisfaction at the total bag of some two hundred snipe did much to smooth matters over. Indeed, the bag would have been still larger except for the vile shooting of one gun; but as a few days later his engagement to one of the ladies of the tiffin-party was announced, the mystery was explained, and when in a few weeks the wedding bells rang, we all forgave him.

Four or five miles outside the principal gate of Peking is the Nan Hai-tzu, or Imperial Hunting Park, where a few years ago there were herds of far-famed hybrids known as the "four unlikes," since they possessed certain attributes of, I believe, the horse, the deer, the ox and the sheep, without belonging definitely to either family. Unfortunately, Europeans were not allowed to enter this preserve, so I was unable personally to see these curiosities, although their existence was well authenticated.

Outside the lofty wall enclosing this park is a kind of common interspersed with marshland through which a small stream flows, and there I have bagged as many as ten couple of snipe in an afternoon, with an occasional wild duck.

Sending out the cart with gun, dog and provisions in charge of the head mafoo at about eleven o'clock on Saturday morning, as soon as work was over at one I would mount my pony, held in readiness by the second mafoo, and gallop with him after the cart, to find tiffin awaiting me spread on the grass.

In this way I was comfortably ready to shoot by half-past two, which would allow of about two and a half hours' sport before returning.

On one of these occasions I saw several large flocks of sand grouse, which, I believe, are native to Mongolia, but only once managed to get within range, killing a brace. They are beautiful, gamey-looking birds, of a very light brown or sand colour, mottled on the back and with legs and feet thickly feathered. Their flight much resembles that of golden plover, only sharper.

Having finished shooting, my gun was again placed in the cart and we started leisurely for home, I riding a short distance in advance, followed by the second mafoo, while my pointer rambled over the grass. One evening, when thus returning, two medium-sized eagles swooped at the dog and commenced to regularly hunt him, much to his consternation. To dismount and get my gun out of its case again was the work of a couple of minutes, when I shot one of the birds at a distance of twenty yards, the other, instead of being alarmed, immediately swooping at its fallen comrade, to meet with a similar fate.

I could not get them stuffed, so had their wings and claws mounted as fans, which I still have somewhere in my possession.

The common deer are small, from thirty to forty pounds in weight, and without horns. They have a thick, bristly hide, and the buck has two tusks of from two to four inches in length projecting downwards from the upper jaw, with which he tears up the ground in search of roots, and it is to these peculiarities that the name of "hog-deer" is due. They mostly lie in the grass on forms, like hares, but sometimes in thick scrub on the hillside, and can be knocked over at forty yards with pheasant shot. I have bagged four in a day more than once. If well cooked the venison is delicious.

Partridges are only found in certain districts. A few miles from Chefoo excellent sport is to be had, but in Central China they are not often seen, although they do exist, as I have shot one myself near Ngankin. Down south the bamboo partridge abounds in places, but it is a very different bird from the ordinary partridge, and takes its name from the fact that it lives, moves and has its being in bamboo coppices.

In the vicinity of Hongkong and Macao the partridge, although far from numerous, is quite common, and a bag of three or four would represent a good day's work. These birds resemble the red-legged variety so common in England, but are considerably larger, while the plumage, although practically identical in colour, is far more brilliant. A curious feature about them is that they are never flushed in coveys and very rarely in pairs, but are almost invariably single birds, which fact, together with their large size and gorgeous plumage, leads me to think that they must represent a distinct branch of the family, to which the name "solitary" would be highly applicable.

Quail are numerous and in all respects resemble those found in this country. They are chiefly prized by the Chinese for their pugilistic qualities, for after being caught and having had their wings clipped they are disposed of to various purchasers, who take them to miniature cock-pits and there back them to fight the birds of other gamblers for considerable sums, the combats being fierce and often deadly.

The hares are wretched little animals, all bones and felt, and not larger than the English rabbit. They usually lie in the open, though often found in graves and in holes in the rocks, from which I have thought that they might be the "coney" mentioned in Scripture.

Bustards, or wild turkeys, are found at certain periods all over China. They are very shy, always settle on wide plains, and are extremely difficult of approach--a shot being only obtainable after long and careful stalking.

Although tigers are occasionally to be found in most of the southern provinces, there are but few places easily accessible to Europeans where they exist in any number, and not having been in one of these favoured spots I have had no opportunity to try my hand at this exciting sport, but a friend of mine, who has earned considerable fame at it, and who keeps a row of grinning tiger skulls on his drawing-room mantelpiece as mementoes of successful hunts, described to me how operations are conducted.

At Amoy, which is probably the best known of these districts, when natives from the surrounding country bring word into the settlement that a tiger has been seen, preparations for the hunt are quickly completed, and a party of sportsmen repairs to the scene of action.

The country being exceedingly rocky, the tigers make their lairs in caves and rocks, approached by long tunnels or holes just large enough to admit the beasts, so that to get them out is both difficult and dangerous.

Having traced spore to the entrance of one of these tunnels, my friend crawled in first with his rifle, immediately after him coming a native shikarri, who thrust forward over my friend's back a long bamboo bearing at the end a lighted torch. Next followed three more shikarries, holding long spears, which they similarly thrust in advance, so that the attacking force consisted of a torch, three spears, the Englishman with his rifle and four shikarries, in which order they slowly crept along the passage, the sides of which were worn smooth by continual friction of tigers passing to and fro, until growls and snarls proclaimed that their quarry was near at hand.

Presently two green, shifting eyes could be distinguished a few feet beyond the torch, when, carefully aimed between them, a hollow, express bullet crashed through the monster's skull, killing him on the spot.

What would happen in case the brute was only wounded and charged I have never heard, but personally I should be somewhat chary in trusting to the protection of a torch and three spears.

It is related that a practical old Yankee sport, desirous of slaying his tiger, joined in one of these expeditions, setting out from the rendezvous armed to the teeth, in company with another hunter, but before very long came stepping briskly back, and by way of explanation guessed "the tiger's footprints were getting too durned fresh."

I consider he showed true American acumen.

Spear-grass one often hears of but seldom sees, and until making acquaintance with the real thing I had always imagined that the barbed grass seeds, which are such a harmful worry to dogs, were practically identical with it. Not at all.

Before leaving Ichang for a trip to the Yangtse gorges I expressed my intention of trying to get some of those beautiful Reeves pheasants, having tails several feet in length, which are indigenous to that locality, but was warned that it would be necessary to take long leggings as a protection against spear-grass. Not having any with me, and believing I knew what spear-grass was, I refrained from borrowing, so that on landing at Nantou with my dog and gun, it was in an ordinary shooting suit and worsted stockings.

Inquiries of natives as to the whereabouts of these birds soon led me up the mountain-side to a rocky plateau, which looked extremely likely, and where I even saw traces of them. My dog commenced to work, and I followed him into the light, dry, crackling grass, but suddenly became conscious of a smarting in the legs as though walking through nettles, and noticed that the grass was adhering to my stockings. However, I pushed on, my dog being hot on the scent, but presently we both came to a standstill--I, because of cramp in both legs, each of which was now enveloped in grass to the size of a bee-hive; while the dog's shaggy coat had collected it till he appeared as large as a sheep, and could no longer force his way along, besides being in much pain.

It was a short half mile down hill to the boat but the difficulty and discomfort of getting there were considerable. When at length the boy proceeded to take my stockings off it was found that they were practically sewn to my skin by the spear-grass, the tiny barbed points of which had passed in hundreds through the wool and worked like fish-hooks into my calves. Without penetrating deep enough to more than slightly draw blood, they had one and all to be forcibly dragged out as the stockings were peeled off. For days I was lame and sore, while my dog lived in misery for weeks. I did not even see a Reeves pheasant.

At Nantou I gathered delicious oranges from the tree for one cash each, or, eight oranges for a farthing.

A twelve-bore is the best gun for use in China, from the fact that cartridges are everywhere procurable, whereas for other sizes they have frequently to be imported from home, although I must admit that a twenty-bore is preferable for snipe-shooting in warm weather, owing to the lightness of both gun and cartridges.

It seems to be the general opinion, with which I agree, that pointers and spaniels are the most suitable dogs to keep, for they appear to work the cover and to stand the climate better than other breeds.

As European dogs seldom live in China more than three or four years, and often less, it is necessary to always have puppies coming on if you do not want your shooting to be spoiled, for it is useless to try and get pheasants out of the thick cover without them. Dysentery is a very prevalent canine disease, but their most deadly enemy, and one existing in no other country that I know of, is worms in the heart. How the germs get into the blood no doctor has yet been able to say, but thin, white worms resembling vermicelli cluster round the heart, living on the blood, until they become so numerous as to eventually choke an artery, when death is instantaneous. In the case of a favourite dog, on which a doctor kindly performed a post-mortem examination, these worms were in such numbers that I positively could not see the heart at all.

Native dogs are useless for sport, as they seem to be devoid of that friendly intelligence so noticeable in our own breeds, while their powers of scent are much inferior. I have heard that in the island of Hainan a certain breed exists which is very good for hunting leopards and wild boar, but this I cannot guarantee.

In the winter of 1889 I was invited by a friend to join him in his house-boat a few miles below Chinkiang, when we could shoot together next day and then have Christmas dinner on board.

I hired a small sampan to sail me down, together with my boy, taking only a bottle of whisky, a few things for tiffin and a plum cake, the last being a Christmas gift from a Norwegian lady.

Starting at noon, it was about three o'clock and near the rendezvous, when we sighted a flock of geese asleep in the sun on a mud-bank. I ordered the sampan-man to get as near as possible, and when the geese rose at a distance of about sixty yards, knocked down a couple with two charges of S.S.G. A minute later another came flying overhead calling to its wounded mate, and this also I dropped without pity. The first two, being only winged, gave a lot of trouble, as they swam and dived with great speed, but all three were eventually secured.

There was still an hour before dark, and seeing no signs of my friend I went on shore and bagged three pheasants before returning to the boat. Next morning, after passing a cold and miserable night in the tiny cabin of the dirty little sampan, I started with gun and dog at about eight o'clock--fully expecting that the house-boat would turn up during my absence--and shot all day, killing eleven pheasants, two deer, three woodcock, seven duck and one pigeon. As by dark there were still no signs of my expected host I had no choice but to return home.

It was a lovely night, bright, frosty and star-light, with a nice, crisp breeze, which, the river being there about two miles wide, raised quite a sea. Thousands of wildfowl, all on their way south, were flying, whistling and whirring about in every direction, and rising from the water quite close to the boat. My dog "Snipe" and I crept into the cabin out of the cutting wind, which was dead ahead, and proceeded to discuss our impromptu Christmas fare, which, after all, was not so bad, and reflected great credit on the boy's cooking powers. I noted down the menu, and here it is:--

1. Pigeon Soup. 2. Woodcock. 3. Boiled Pheasant. 4. Cold Roast Beef. 5. Plum Cake ablaze with Whisky. 6. Cheese. 7. Pumelo. Whisky and Water. Tea.

There was no holly or mistletoe to remind one of Merrie England, but I drank to "the Old Folks at Home" with the sadness peculiar to wanderers on such occasions, and then gave myself up to nicotine and reflection for the rest of the evening, arriving home at midnight to find that my truant friend was ill in bed.

CHAPTER IV

RIDING

No country in the world is so badly supplied with horses as China, both as regards quantity and quality.

The reasons for this are largely owing to the peculiar and wretched condition of internal communications, and to the fact that horses are seldom employed in cultivation of the soil, which is mostly performed by manual labour, supplemented by water buffaloes in the central and southern provinces and by oxen in the north.

Wherever rivers and lakes exist there is found a dense boating population, whose occupation is the conduct of every kind of traffic.

On the large fluvial highways stately junks laden deep with cargo pass backwards and forwards in unending procession. In shallower waters the vessels are smaller but more numerous, and this adaptation to circumstances goes on until the smallest streams and canals, which invariably cover the valleys of China's mighty rivers as with a net, are blocked with tiny craft, each bearing its load of merchandise or its quota of passengers.

In such districts, where everything is carried by water and where roads are few, there is little or no work for the horse, which, beyond a few wretched specimens attached to the various yam 阯 s and military camps, is seldom seen.

Where waterways do not exist, and traffic must necessarily be carried overland, the highways are either narrow paths paved with large blocks of stone and suitable only for wheelbarrows and pack-animals, or tracks picked out at random over a width of perhaps a hundred yards, along which lumbering, ill-constructed and springless carts plough their ways, and strings of pack-animals wend slowly to and fro. The numberless creaking wheelbarrows, bearing heavy loads, are propelled by coolies, who, the yoke across the shoulders, stagger along between the shafts, helped occasionally by a small sail set to catch a favouring wind, or by another coolie harnessed to the vehicle by ropes. The pack-animals mostly consist of camels (especially in the north), mules and donkeys, ponies being used in more limited numbers. As a rule, the carts are supplied with mixed teams of very poor class animals, mules largely predominating, although ponies are also numerous.

Europeans, accustomed to see carriages, dog-carts and all kinds of horse-drawn conveyances circulating freely on macadamised roads, find it difficult to realise that, in the oldest civilised empire in existence, there are, outside the treaty-ports, not only no macadamised roads, but not even roads that could possibly be compared with our most out-of-the-way and most ill-kept country lanes, and that consequently there are neither carriages nor dogcarts, but only springless tumbrils, which, covered with a wain, discharge the functions of the celestial cab, and plough through deep mud with their massive wheels, or jolt over stone causeways to the intense discomfort of luckless occupants.

There being then practically neither roads nor carriages, the demand for draught horses is very small, while for riding purposes Chinamen prefer either the taller and more dignified mule or the ambling pony.

This latter has a rolling, pacing gait which enables the horseman to sit quietly in his high wooden saddle without any necessity of rising in the stirrups. He possesses great speed and endurance, and wealthy Chinese will give as much as four or five hundred taels for a good one. With his rider leaning well back and pulling hard at the reins the animal tears along at fifteen or sixteen miles an hour, but when the reins are loosened he immediately slackens and pulls up. They are a common sight in the neighbourhood of Peking, where ambling contests frequently take place outside the city wall. In these contests each pony in turn is ridden at full speed past the judges, who proclaim the winner on his general merits and not with exclusive reference to pace.

For agricultural work the horse is not employed. In wheeling barrows coolies perform the work of beasts of burthen. As pack-animals camels, mules and donkeys have the preference, so that although the "noble animal" is to be met with almost everywhere, he is not considered indispensable as in Western lands. He is unhonoured, ill cared for and very cheap.

There may be several breeds in China, although personally I have seen but four, of which a small, well-shaped pony from Turkestan; a large, stringy horse from Ili; and a weedy, cowhocked pony from Szechuan deserve here no more than passing notice, for they are seldom seen in the Eastern provinces, where alone the Mongolian, or, as it is commonly called, the "China pony," is found in considerable numbers.

This China pony, with which Europeans in the Far East are so well acquainted, is a native of the Mongolian plains. He stands on an average about thirteen hands, and is a coarse, thick-set, cobby animal, with a large, ugly head carried low on a wedge-shaped neck, so that when mounted you have practically nothing in front of the saddle. He much resembles, and is evidently closely allied to, the Russian pony, which is now so commonly met with in this country.

I have heard it stated that, at the conclusion of the Second Chinese War, to avoid the expense of transport back to India, the Arab horses of our cavalry were sold at Tientsin, and being mostly purchased by native dealers, were sent to Mongolia and crossed with the native breed. If this be true it accounts for the traces of Arab blood which may occasionally be observed in a smaller head, finer points, wavy tail and gentler manners.

Mongol princes have long had, by imperial decree, the sole right of horse breeding in the north, every year paying tribute to the Emperor of so many head; and as this breed is much superior to the others I have mentioned, the monopoly practically extends to the whole Empire, and is most jealously guarded.

Geldings only are allowed to leave the breeders' hands, and that not before the advanced age of seven or eight, which partly accounts for the shortness of the time during which China ponies are in their prime, and for the fact that after two or three years' work they commence to age and deteriorate.

Mares it is impossible to purchase on any terms, the Mongols absolutely refusing to part with them, and I have only seen two during the whole of the twelve years I have spent in China--one at Peking, the property of a Russian prince, and one with its foal, belonging to a native official at Kiukiang.

In the late autumn of every year the tribute ponies are brought down to Peking. I have seen them in large droves coming across country at full gallop, enveloped in clouds of dust, with mounted Mongol and Chinese drovers, carrying long bamboo poles, riding on the outskirts of each mob and directing its course. Villagers, on seeing the clouds of dust and hearing the thunder of hoofs, hurry out to try and divert the equine torrent from their crops, but in vain. The whirlwind rushes by, leaving a broad, well-beaten track, whereon few signs of banks, gardens or vegetation can be discerned. It is the Emperor's tribute and there is no redress.

After tributary obligations have been fulfilled in kind or in value, large numbers of these ponies are thrown on the market, and on an average can be secured for twenty or thirty dollars each--that is, for two or three pounds.

The best market is provided by Europeans, and dealers forward the finest-looking animals to Tientsin, Shanghai, Hongkong, Hankow and other places where racing is carried on, to meet this demand.

When such mobs of raw ponies reach a treaty-port they are known as "griffins," which term applies to all that have not previously run at any race-meeting; and with their tails sweeping the ground, their hogged manes and their long coats clotted with mud, they present a very dismal appearance, and one not at all in keeping with the accepted idea of race-horses.

These griffins mostly pass through the hands of racing men, who, with a view to securing a good animal, either arrange with the dealers for private gallops, when the various performances are carefully timed by stop-watch, or buy their fancies at public auction without speed tests having previously been made.

Owing to expenses of transport, be it by steamer or by road, the further south the greater the average value of griffins, and as only picked animals are supplied to the foreign market, the price is everywhere far higher than at Peking, and may be said to range from fifty to five hundred dollars. Those ponies which do not prove to have sufficient speed to warrant their being trained as racers are resold as hacks, or filter away at lower prices to the Chinese.

I may here say that although at several of the treaty-ports there are a few good roads made by the European residents, and along which imported carriages are occasionally seen to pass, it is only at Shanghai that vehicular traffic has attained to any considerable degree of importance. Here the foreign settlements are traversed in all directions by excellent highways, which extend through the suburbs for several miles into the adjoining country, and which the Chinese avail themselves of to a large extent, driving out in thousands every afternoon to tea-houses and pleasure-gardens.

Besides most well-known varieties of conveyance the celestial mind has evolved one or two remarkable models of its own, notably, a kind of victoria, the body of which takes the form of two large inverted sea-shells gaudily painted with flowers and butterflies, and running on light iron wheels with bright spokes and rubber tyres. A liveried coach-man on the box, a footman with a smart rug over the arm standing on an iron step behind and balancing himself by grasping two straps attached to the back corners of the carriage, a shabbily-harnessed China pony in the shafts, and the equipage is complete.

The occupants of this triumphal car are either three or four prosperous-looking Chinamen, clothed in many-coloured silks, or a posse of gaily-dressed celestial beauties, who, with faces painted white, lips dyed vermilion, hair caked with oil, garlanded with flowers, laden with jewels, displaying their tiny satin shoes and toying with fans in their small and beautiful hands, furnish a tout-ensemble sufficiently original if not too painfully grotesque.

At Shanghai, certainly, many thousands of ponies are employed, but it is owing entirely to the influence and example of Europeans.

The majority of men taking up appointments in China are barely out of, if not still in, their teens, and whether they come straight from school, from business in the city or from the universities, it is seldom they have had any large experience of horses. In very many cases they do not even know how to mount, but finding ponies so cheap, or, better still, getting a discarded racer as a cumshaw, they take to riding as naturally as if to the manner born, so that there are but few residents of either sex who cannot ride, and China ponies consequently hold a place in the estimation of foreigners which is altogether denied them by the natives.

From hacking to racing is but a step. The man who has learnt to ride (or thinks he has), being already a member of the race club, takes his steed for a quiet canter round the course. The old racer no sooner finds himself on the familiar track than he is off with the speed of flames, and our young friend, being powerless to check him, with his feet out of the stirrups and hanging on to the back of the saddle for dear life, is carried a mile or so before a sudden swerve at the exit rail deposits him on the turf.

No bones are broken but the damage is done. Unless the dismounted cavalier be devoid of all enthusiasm the spirit of racing has assuredly entered his veins!

In future he will haunt the course with his own luckless hack, he will attend the training regularly each morning in hopes of getting a mount on any rank outsider, and will think of little else all day than riding and ponies.

To some men riding comes naturally, like cricket, while others can never acquire a good seat.

A light-weight who is fortunate enough to possess the necessary knack will soon be in request as jockey at the forthcoming meeting, when, if he should happen to secure a win, the confidence it immediately gives him does more than any other thing to transform him into a really good horseman.

It costs no more to feed a good pony than it does a bad one, so he now decides to dispose of his hack for a trifling sum, and in its stead to purchase a griffin, which may be a potential winner of the champions. He orders his mafoo to inspect the new season's griffins as they arrive, and arrange with the dealer to bring three or four of the best for his approval. This the mafoo does with great pleasure, as, apart from the keen interest he takes in racing-- all Chinese being inveterate gamblers--it is an understood thing that he will receive a good cumshaw from his master for each race that his stable wins.

In due course the unbroken, shoeless, mud-covered animals arrive, and the dealer, perched on a high wooden saddle, trots them up and down to show off their paces.

In England the would-be purchaser of a horse carefully feels each leg to make sure that there be neither splint nor curb, lifts up and examines the hoofs, grasps the lower lip with one hand and draws out the tongue with the other to study the teeth, and peers closely into the animal's face to see that his eyes are unblemished.

On approaching a griffin one becomes conscious of being closely watched by a vicious eye, and oftentimes the brute, snorting with anger and alarm at the unaccustomed sight and smell of a European, attempts to rush at one, while the idea of feeling his legs, drawing out his tongue, examining his hoofs or peering into his eyes quickly evaporates. One would rather fondle a Bengal tiger!

An adjournment is next made to the race-course, where the ponies are powed by the dealer for half-a-mile, when the action of each can be observed and the times taken by stop-watch.

In this manner a rough idea can be formed as to which of the animals are likely to possess the necessary turn of speed, and that is as much information as can now be obtained, for as to soundness, age and stamina the dealer's assurances on these points must be accepted as the only evidence procurable.

In the end one, and very probably two, are purchased at from sixty to seventy dollars each, and the erstwhile embryo jock has blossomed into the dignity of ownership.

The first thing to do with a griffin is to get him shod, which is not quite so simple a matter as one might imagine, for he has hitherto never passed through the farrier's hands and will be certain to fiercely object. No attempt is made to perform the operation by gentleness, and he is forthwith led under a kind of oblong, wooden arch about six feet high, constructed of four firmly-planted posts, connected on top by cross beams.

Ropes passed under his belly and over the cross beams keep him from throwing himself down, while each leg is securely lashed to one of the posts, and thus being rendered absolutely powerless, the work is quickly put through.

There is generally a struggle in mounting each new arrival, but with a couple of mafoos hanging on to his ears, and sometimes by enveloping his head in a horse-cloth, it is eventually managed.

The first timidity soon wears off, and you find that after a short distance there is no more trouble, the animal being probably in poor condition and lacking the nervousness of finer breeds.

Several days of scraping and grooming having removed the dust and dirt with which his shaggy coat was filled, he is clipped and his tail shortened. The transformation is almost startling. You now have quite a smart-looking mount as China ponies go, and while riding him daily to improve his condition you will soon discover any marked characteristics.

He rarely gets over his dislike for Europeans although perfectly docile with Chinese, and it is seldom that he will allow even his own master to enter the stall. A black griffin which I bought at Peking seemed to me so quiet that on an expedition of some days into the country I fed, groomed and saddled him myself, until quite convinced that we had become friends, and it was not till after my return that, in passing through the stables, he rushed at me with open mouth, only the strength of a raw-hide headstall saving me from being savaged.

What applies to one applies to all. Their tempers are untrustworthy.

Many have the disagreeable trick of "cow-kicking," which usually occurs on mounting, when they kick forward with the near hind leg and may inflict a nasty blow.

Invariably hard-mouthed, occasionally buck-jumpers, altogether without manners, and in trotting mostly slow and jerky, they are but a poor apology for the gentle and graceful horse as found in Western countries. On the other hand, they make capital race-ponies, for they are fast gallopers, and for their size can carry astounding weights. They are also very good for cross-country work, as, in addition to being fair jumpers, their great strength enables them to plough through country which would tax the powers of an English hunter, but the greatest consideration of all is their cheapness, for it places them within the reach of sporting men with small incomes.

A certain number of Australian horses are now imported into Hongkong and Shanghai, but owing to the stringencies of the Chinese climate it is very doubtful whether so great additional outlay as the long sea voyage involves is compensated for by the walers' evident superiorities.

Assuming that, having had a griffin for some time, he is in good condition, a period of six or seven weeks is sufficient in which to prepare him for the races.

For training purposes, oats and hay imported from California are preferable, but adhering to native produce, a diet of boiled barley, chopped straw and bran will do nearly as well.

Most of the important exercise is gone through at early morning between six and half-past seven, when the ponies are trotted and galloped on the course, and when all sporting members of the community, stop-watch in hand, assemble at the rails, or follow proceedings from the grand-stand while breakfasting on hot rolls and coffee. On return to stables, thorough dressing, with much rubbing of the legs, takes place, while an hour's brisk walking from eleven o'clock to twelve, and again in the afternoon, completes the day's work.

Each animal requires individual treatment, and it is the owner who best knows how to apply it that will bring his ponies to the post in the fittest condition.

Carrying from ten to eleven stone according to measurement, good time for half a mile would be fifty-nine seconds, for a mile, two minutes eight seconds, and for a mile and a half, three minutes fifteen seconds.

In dry weather it is an advantage for ponies to race without shoes, but if the course be wet or muddy they are absolutely necessary to prevent slipping.

The jockeys are all amateur and mostly personal friends, as also are the clerk of the course, starters, judges and stewards, so that instead of a race-meeting being a gathering of complete strangers, bookmakers and professionals, it partakes more of the social nature of a huge picnic.

During the winter months a great feature of sport in Shanghai is paperchasing on horseback.

The meets are usually held on Saturday afternoons, when business offices are closed, and a field of seventy or eighty is no uncommon sight.

Two members of the club lay the scent, but while free to choose any line of country, they must not lead the trail over jumps or obstacles which their own ponies have failed to negotiate.

At the hour advertised the Master gives a signal and the hunt is away.

Through wades and creeks, over water-jumps and graves, across gardens and paddy fields, the gay throng sweeps on at high speed, until a welcome check brings relief to man and beast and allows the stragglers to close up. After a short delay the trail is again hit off and the field streams away, but in ever-decreasing numbers, until a mere handful sight the flags which mark the finish, and ride their hardest at the final jump, the first light-weight and the first welter to cross which are thereafter entitled to sport pink and gain the honour of laying scent for the succeeding hunt. The sport is extremely good though very rough, which is mainly owing to the marshy nature of the soil and the fact that as the Chinese do not here raise banks or hedges between their fields the jumping is mostly over water and dry ditches of considerable width and depth, which accounts for a goodly number of nasty spills. Although compensation for damage to crops is awarded by the hunt club, considerable care must be taken to guard against traps wilfully laid by the natives, who frequently remove the trail from its proper course and lay it over almost impossible jumps, which they further render extremely dangerous by digging holes in the opposite banks and covering them with leaves and rubbish, after doing which they take up safe positions of vantage to enjoy the fun.

In autumn, when the waters of the Yangtse commence to fall and the inundated districts along its banks become dry, the plain at Hankow affords excellent riding, where for miles one can swing along at a hand-gallop without once having to draw rein. In spring, when covered with fresh, green grass, it possesses an additional charm, and until rising waters once more confine riding to the race-course and the river bank, there are few places in China where such magnificent gallops can be obtained.

When summer floods at Kiukiang drove our ponies from their mat stables on the other side of the creek to the higher ground of the concession, and turned most of the surrounding country into an immense lake, we were in considerable perplexity as to where we should take our afternoon rides, until the brilliant idea was conceived of utilising the city wall, which stands about twenty feet in height, and is four miles in circumference.

Entering by the western gate and turning sharply to the right we rode up the stone steps, much worn by time and human feet, to the top of the wall, which is some twelve feet in width. Picking our way carefully, for the route was strewn with loose stones and bricks, we usually made the circuit twice before descending. Where the steps adjoin the wall two large right angles are formed, into which Chinese houses have been built in such a manner that their roofs are conterminous with, and slope at the same angle as, the steps, rendering it possible to pass from one to the other with the greatest of ease.

As a friend of mine was passing this point for the second time his pony tried to bolt down the steps with the intention of returning to stable. A violent pull at the near rein brought the brute's head round, but without stopping him, so that he passed sideways from the steps on to the roof of one of the houses, and together with his rider instantly disappeared through it, amidst a cloud of dust, a crashing of timbers and the rattle of falling tiles.

Emerging from the debris, and smothered with dust, my friend led his pony through the front door into the street, where a crowd had already collected, neither apparently any the worse for their remarkable feat. An old woman who was in the building at the time had a narrow escape from being crushed by the falling animal, but she soon recovered from the shock, and a liberal sum in dollars with which to repair the roof probably caused her to regret that similar accidents did not more frequently befall.

At Peking, where for a time I was clerk of the course, a most remarkable incident occurred, for the accuracy of which I had irrefutable proof.

A pony named "Chalk," which I had purchased from a Chinese soldier for twenty-five dollars, had carried all before him at the previous autumn meeting, for which reason I was naturally greatly attached to him, and he, although an extremely vicious animal towards others, tolerated me with a forbearance but rarely met with in a China pony.

At the succeeding spring meeting Chalk was a hot favourite for the principal events. The evening before the races I passed with several friends, when the chances of different ponies, and of Chalk in particular, were discussed till a late hour. That night I dreamed that after I had been riding Chalk, I was standing dismounted and holding the reins, on a plot of grass surrounded with trees, while the pony was lying on the ground. Raising his head and neck two or three times in attempts to get up he finally struggled into a sitting position, standing on his forelegs but with his haunches on the ground, and then sank back dead.

The dream was so vivid and left such an impression on me, that by way of conversation, and without attaching the slightest importance to it, I related the circumstance in practically the same words as employed here, to a Russian friend, who accompanied me early next morning to the course.

Again, on the grand-stand, a quarter of an hour or so before the races commenced, I laughingly told a son of the Dutch minister of my dream, explaining the circumstances and the scene in full.

Looking in the pink of condition, Chalk came out for the first event, one mile, and won hands down by several lengths. After dismounting in the enclosure and weighing in, I was being convoyed by my friends to the bar in order to celebrate the victory in champagne, when I heard someone say, "Look at Chalk!"

Turning round, I saw him staggering backwards as if he had been struck a heavy blow on the head. As I rushed forward and seized the reins by which the mafoo had been leading him, he fell to the ground, and there on the club lawn, surrounded with trees, exactly as seen in my dream, he attempted to rise two or three times, eventually getting into a sitting position, and then falling back was dead in less than ten seconds.

My Russian friend was aghast, and pressed into my hand a small coin, which he said would keep off the evil spirits, but I was then too much concerned at the loss of my favourite to pay heed to either spirits or dreams, although I had instantly recognised both the scene and the locality, the only difference being that the sympathising crowd which now pressed round me and my fallen steed had been absent in the vision.

I am not a believer in dreams, and possessing an excellent digestion but rarely have any, and for this one can offer no explanation beyond that it was a most remarkable coincidence.

At the time it created quite a mild sensation amongst the European community, while the Chinese who heard of it were extremely interested.

My Russian and Dutch friends I have since met on several occasions, when, in the presence of others, we talked of my dream and its fulfilment.

Both in Peking and in the various parts of China where I have since been stationed, I have frequently related the occurrence to Chinese acquaintances, and they have always given an interpretation of it which has invariably been to the effect that in this world, or in a previous existence, I either lent money or did a great service to some friend, who, dying before repayment had been made, came back to earth in the form of a horse, and after winning for me sufficient money to discharge his debt, returned to the realms of departed spirits.

"THE HAGUE, "26th March 1903.

"MY DEAR READY,--In reply to yours of 23rd I will certainly gladly corroborate the incident regarding Chalk's death. I do not remember exactly the details as you put them to me now, though I have not the least doubt they were the true features of the case. What I do still remember is this: that you gave ---- and myself a somewhat circumstantial account of your dream shortly before the race; that immediately after the death of the pony you came up to us and called attention to the remarkable fulfilment of your dream, and that I was at the time much impressed with the case, both as regards the main fact and the details, which tallied remarkably with what I could then still remember of your prophetic account of the event. Whether to look upon this as some 'Borderland' manifestation or merely as a remarkable coincidence does not belong to the province of,--

"Yours very truly,

"T.T.H. FERGUSON."

My Russian friend has long since returned to the dominions of the Great White Czar and I have not his address, otherwise I feel confident that he, too, would gladly support with his testimony my account of this remarkable occurrence.

CHAPTER V

SAILING

A good national motto for the Chinese would be "Semper idem," for of a truth they change not and as yet the shadow of turning is but ill-defined.

The same types of junk that called forth the admiration of Marco Polo may be seen to-day, not only along the internal waterways of the Empire but far afield, at Singapore, in Siamese waters and amongst the East India Islands, and it may be interesting for yachtsmen to know that the problems of water-tight compartments, centre-boards, balanced and perforated rudders, which during the past few decades have exercised the minds of designers and builders in this country, were solved many centuries ago by the Chinese, and almost every junk afloat contains some, and not unfrequently all, of these equipments.

In the stormy waters of the Formosa channel, where the monsoons raise a mountainous sea, thousands of fishing-boats, far out of sight of land, ply their business in weather which would cause the masters of English smacks to run for shelter.

Mail steamers on the voyage between Hongkong and Shanghai pass through these fleets and their miles upon miles of bamboo-floated nets, and oftentimes it occurs that a good view of some of the craft may be obtained from deck at the distance of only a few yards, when it can be seen that their crews consist not of men alone as in other countries but of whole families-- fathers, mothers, children and infants--whose home is in reality on the rolling deep.

That many of these hardy souls perish at their work is a certainty, for it frequently happens that steamers sight their luckless craft bottoms upwards or rescue survivors from the wreckage.

Out of Shanghai harbour cumbersome junks make their ways across the Yellow Sea to ports along the northern coasts or to the hermit kingdom of Corea. These vessels have frequently five or six masts spread out like a fan, from the foremast, which rakes forrard at an extraordinary angle, to the mizzenmast, which shoots well out over the stern. Ill-shaped sails of matting, ropes made of twisted bamboo splits, hemp, or cocoa-nut fibre, huge wooden anchors, and a total absence of paint lend to them a most ramshackle and unseaworthy appearance, while clothes drying on the line, cocks crowing, pigs rambling about at will, plants growing in pots and old tins, together with the presence of women and children, introduce a rustic and farmlike element, and it is always a matter of wonder to me how these floating curiosity shops are able to thread their ways unaided through tortuous channels and crowded shipping out to sea, and when once there, why they do not succumb to the first rough weather they encounter.

Taken as a whole, Chinese junks are but roughly built, and though generally excellent sea-boats and easily handled, their sailing powers are poor when compared with corresponding European craft of similar tonnage.

A peculiar custom is the supplying of all vessels, whether steamers, junks or sampans, with large eyes, which are painted one on either side of the bows and as a reason for which any Chinaman will explain to you--"S'pose no got eye, no can see. S'pose no can see, how fashion can walkee."

Another thing to be noted is that all sails without exception have bamboo reefing battens, which although destroying the smooth set of the canvas are infinitely superior to our reefing points, inasmuch as the largest sail can be reefed from deck, or rather reefs itself, just as quickly as the capstan can lower it, and without that hard work, waste of time and risk which going aloft or along the spars in bad weather necessarily entails.

Up the mighty River Yangtse different types of junks may be numbered by the hundred, all varying in tonnage, dimensions and draught according to the waters they are designed to navigate.

[Illustration: FOOCHOW JUNK, SHOWING EYE. To face page 98.]

In the estuary, and as far up as Chinkiang, sea-going papicoes from Ningpo are to be seen in great numbers. These gaily-painted vessels of from twenty to eighty tons, with their high freeboards, wide sterns, raking masts, tanned sails and gaudy vanes, are extremely quaint and picturesque.

Via the Grand Canal, which connects Tientsin with Hangchow, great quantities of tribute rice are forwarded by Chinese officials from the Central and Southern provinces to their Manchu rulers in the north, every Manchu, owing to the bare fact that he is of the ruling race, being entitled from his birth to a monthly allowance of rice and silver, and as the canal crosses the Yangtse at Chinkiang many deep-draught grain junks may be seen arriving there with cargoes from various places on the river.

A few miles higher up, at a place called Iching, there are always scores of junks anchored in orderly rows waiting to load salt as it arrives overland from the sea-coast, where, being a Government monopoly, it is manufactured in saltpans under official supervision.

Both the grain junks and the salt junks possess a certain official status, and are therefore kept in far better trim than the ordinary trader, and ranging anywhere from sixty to one hundred and fifty tons, are probably the best class of craft which frequent inland waters. They are heavily built, with good beam and watertight compartments. Their lines, while forbidding any thought of speed, are not ungraceful, and eminently suitable for weight carrying. With square, massive bows they thicken away aft, until, curving upwards with a bold sweep of the gunnels, their covered-in sterns, high above the balanced rudder, form good quarters for the lowdah and his family, where from tiny windows women and children peep in shy curiosity at the foreigner sailing by.

The mainmast, an enormous spar of some sixty or seventy feet in length, is stepped almost amidships in a kind of tabernacle, and has neither stays nor shrouds, its only visible support being a wooden prop, which a few feet above the deck takes part of the pressure when running before the wind, so that on gazing up at its dizzy height one continually wonders why in heavy weather it does not go by the board or pound its way through the bottom of the vessel. The foremast, which is considerably smaller and stepped well forrard, is in like manner devoid of any kind of stay. Each mast sets one enormous sail of graceful shape, and but loosely made of a coarse, native material, resembling cheap calico. The cloths, running vertically, are interwoven with the bamboo reefing battens, and though but lightly stitched together, seem capable of withstanding an enormous strain.

Varnished a light yellow, which shimmers in the sun, and displaying gaudy banners on which the signs of the guilds to which they belong are printed in large characters, it is a beautiful sight to watch a fleet of these stately ships glide by, with their towering sails goose-winged before the breeze, and churning up the waters with their blunt, unyielding prows.

Amongst the elaborate system of guilds which permeates Chinese society, one of the most meritorious is the lifeboat guild. Apart from official aid and direction, it is mostly supported by voluntary contributions, and to an extent which allows of lifeboats being stationed at many points of danger.

In fine weather these "red-boats," as, owing to their usual colour, they are commonly called, lay up in creeks or shelters while the crews pass their time at leisure, but as soon as a storm arises they immediately put out and ride to a drift-anchor, ready at a moment's notice to hoist sail and dash to the rescue of any craft in distress.

At Hankow, where a north-easterly gale against a four-knot current raises a choppy and heavy sea most dangerous for small craft, I have seen four red-boats racing from different directions to rescue the occupants of a capsized sampan. With sails fully hoisted before the gale and smothered by the waves, in an incredibly short time they were on the scene of the accident, where, rounding to, the work of salvage was carried out in a most plucky and seamanlike manner. These boats have no stem, the bows, which are square and about four feet in width, sloping away underneath in a gentle curve, so that their tendency is to skim over the water like a dish instead of cutting through it. They are decked forrard flush with the gunnel for nearly half their length, when a low cabin takes up the space as far as the well, which is quite aft.

Flat-bottomed, and using lee-boards, they draw very little water, while a single mast and sail of the light and convenient Chinese pattern render them extremely handy. Hand-lines are looped round the sides in the customary manner, but there is no cork belt.

Their qualities are so good that our own National Lifeboat Institution would do well to study the model for use in places where a sandy beach and shoal water make it sometimes impossible to launch the type of lifeboat now in general use.

Gun-boats, or police junks, are ubiquitous. A very low freeboard and no cabin, with the exception of a kind of deck-house quite aft, where the helmsman stands, one mast hoisting a gracefully-cut sail with alternate blue and white cloths, a small muzzle-loading cannon in the bows, and a crew of ten or a dozen in quaint uniforms, who, when wind fails, take to the sweeps, and standing up facing the direction in which they are going, and keeping good time, propel the boat at a fair pace. When at anchor an awning in blue and white stripes affords a commodious shelter. Being official vessels they are spic and span in light yellow varnish, and frequently fly a number of really beautiful flags of marvellous design and brilliant colouring. The tout-ensemble is smart, weird, pleasing and eminently suitable for a Drury Lane pantomime. Of shallow draught, and of size varying in accordance with the waters they are destined to patrol, I have seen them as large as twenty tons and as small as a skiff, having an old flint gingall mounted forrard with all the circumstance of a 12-inch gun.

Between the treaty-port of Ichang, which is a thousand miles from the sea, and the treaty-port of Chungking, which is four hundred miles higher up, lie the celebrated Yangtse Gorges.

Ichang is, for all practical purposes, the present terminus of steamship traffic, for although a few small steamers have passed through the Gorges and reached Chungking, there have been many failures, and one German vessel, the ss. Shuihsiang, built expressly for the run, was dashed on the rocks and sank when on her maiden trip.

The scenery of the Gorges is the grandest I have ever seen, and made a greater impression on me than even that of the Rocky Mountains.

My trip there was in the month of November, when the river was low and the current slack, albeit it raced by at five or six miles an hour.

Having hired a suitable boat at Ichang we set sail before a strong up-river breeze, and by carefully following all indentations of the river bank managed to keep in fairly slack water, until we reached a point where the Gorges actually commence. Here a tow-line was got out, and by the frantic efforts of half-a-dozen trackers, in addition to the sail, we slowly forged ahead but at not more than two miles an hour, although the foam breaking over our bows and a broad wake astern showed that we were passing through the water at the rate of eight or nine.

The Gorges are where the mighty river has forced a passage through a lofty range of mountains, which barred its progress to the sea.

Seated on my tiny craft, and gazing up at the towering cliffs which rise almost perpendicularly for hundreds and sometimes thousands of feet on either side, I could see caves, terraces and strata, which indicate with a marvellous distinctness the different levels of the river, as during untold ages it has eaten its way through solid rock and stone to its present bed. This manifestation of the irresistible forces of nature produces a singularly sobering effect on the mind by making one keenly feel how utterly insignificant we mortals really are. Along ledges on the beetling cliffs the ubiquitous Chinaman has built his home and planted orange groves, so that far overhead rich clusters of golden fruit lend an effective touch of colour to the beauty and majesty of the scene.

All junks in use between Chungking and Ichang are built with a view to navigating the numerous rapids occurring in the Gorges, and are chiefly remarkable for their abnormally high sterns, which, in the event of grounding on a sandbank while descending with a ten-knot current, serve as a protection against being pooped.

One or two masts with the ordinary Chinese sails, an immense sweep in the bows as an aid in turning, and a strong rudder with an enormous tiller, are the chief items of equipment.

On the voyage down, which takes less than a week, a crew of ten or a dozen would be sufficient for a medium-sized junk, but for the return journey against stream, and which takes from four to eight weeks according to the strength of the current, from forty to a hundred trackers are necessary in addition to the regular hands.

As in the Gorges the river is liable to freshets, which in a few hours may cause a rise of thirty or forty feet, the foreshore is at an uncertain height, for which reason, probably, no towing-paths have been made.

Upward-bound junks, in addition to their sails, have an immense hawser, made of twisted bamboo splits, leading from the top of the mainmast to the river bank, and to the shore end of which, for a length of about forty to a hundred feet, the trackers fasten the yokes, with one of which each man is supplied, and which are long enough to admit a play of ten or fifteen feet on either side of the cable.

It is a stirring sight to see a big junk being bodily forced by wind and manual power against a strong current. The trackers swarm over rocks and mounds along the foreshore like a pack of hounds, singing, laughing and shouting as they go, the mainmast bends beneath the heavy strain, the hawser is cleared from jutting boulders by intrepid swimmers, who in pursuit of their vocation must often plunge into the racing torrent, and the vessel roars through the water with foaming bows, though the progress made may be but a few yards within the hour, while if, as frequently occurs, the hawser carries away, she is whirled three or four miles down stream before the crew can again bring her to anchor by the bank.

Wrecks are numerous in this seething maelstrom, and a heavy toll in lives is taken from the brave and hardy fellows whose lot is cast by these waters of strife.

It was on this trip that I saw a Chinaman fishing with the help of an otter.

The animal had a long cord fastened round its neck like a ferret, and was attached by it to the bows of a sampan, which was rowed by a woman, while the fisherman, standing on the fore part, gathered in his hands a net, circular in shape and having a hole in the centre large enough to admit the otter.

On arriving at a suitable spot the net was cast with a sweep of the arm, so that like a spider's web it spread over a considerable area of water.

Heavily weighted at the edges it sank quickly until the leads rested on the bottom of the river. The fisherman then hauled at a line until the hole in the centre appeared above the surface, when the otter, plunging through it, dived inside the net, quickly to reappear with a fish in its mouth, whereon he was unceremoniously hauled on board and his prey taken from him, after which he was again ushered through the hole into the folds of the net.

While stationed at Kiukiang I possessed a teak-built four-oared gig which, being heavy and strong, I rigged with a jib and mainsail, besides adding six inches to her keel, when she proved to be a handy and seaworthy little craft. An iron framework could be erected over the stern-sheets and covered with a canvas hood, thus forming quite a roomy and comfortable cabin, while a light awning protected the well of the boat, so that I was quite able to make trips in her extending over two or three days.

From time to time natives had spoken to me of a Purple Lake where, they said, but few Europeans had ever been, and along the shores of which good shooting could be found.

This sounded sufficiently alluring, so, the opportunity offering, I started on a voyage of discovery in my gig, taking with me a couple of trusty native boatmen. Mounting the Yangtse for a short distance we entered a narrow creek, along which we were carried by a swift current between walls of reeds so tall that they effectually shut off the wind. At dark we tied up near a village, from which dozens of dogs presently arrived, and which when not fighting amongst themselves barked at us throughout the night with the most exasperating persistence. Mosquitoes also were particularly numerous, so that with the first streak of dawn we were only too thankful to cast off and continue our journey. During the morning we passed through pleasant scenery, and I observed a heronry in some dead trees on the left, while a deer swam the creek two hundred yards ahead of the boat; the lake being reached shortly before noon.

It was a refreshing sight. Clear, sparkling water dotted with fishing-boats and wild-fowl, little green-capped islands with white cliffs and a range of lofty mountains in the background. After a swim and a hearty tiffin we sailed on with a good breeze, exploring the different arms of the lake, until about three o'clock, when I landed with my gun.

The country, though hilly, was richly cultivated, the principal crop being tobacco, and after a delightful walk I returned on board with a brace of pheasants and a woodcock. That night we passed in comfort anchored in a tiny bay sheltered by lofty cliffs, and the morning was well aired before our cruise was resumed.

At the further end of the lake what at first appeared to be a stately town was seen rising from the water's edge and reflected on its glistening surface, but a nearer approach revealed the inevitable shabbiness and ruin which distance had concealed and mirage had beautified. A fisherman informed us that it was the "Purple City."

Later on I landed on some low ground, and walking amongst the paddy fields bagged ten couple of snipe in less than an hour, after which we sailed on again up a narrow arm of the lake with beautiful cliffs and wooded hills on either side. Arriving at the end of this inlet we anchored for tiffin, and early in the afternoon commenced to beat back against a northerly wind.

During the morning I had observed a number of boats crossing the lake from all directions and converging on a certain point, and now, on rounding a sharp headland, we suddenly found ourselves in the midst of hundreds of craft of many descriptions, each bearing a load of gaily-dressed holiday-makers, while several long canoes, each paddled by twenty or thirty men, raced backwards and forwards to a great beating of gongs and a firing of guns. It was the dragon-boat festival, and no sooner were we observed than all these boats immediately closed round in order that their occupants might more closely inspect the European and his strange-looking craft.

Far from my presence being resented I was most courteously treated, and after many questions had been put and answered by either side, a race of the dragon-boats was given for my particular edification, while as they sped by I fired a salute from my Winchester, which evidently gave immense satisfaction.

I would here observe that wherever my wanderings in China have led me I have never been molested, nor, beyond the epithet of "foreign devil" applied freely by boys from a safe distance, have I been insulted. While this is not the experience of many, I am obliged to confess that the fault does not lie wholly with the natives.

I have noticed men enter a village with guns, dogs and a tribe of beaters, and to an old inhabitant, who courteously bowed his welcome, one of them shouted roughly, "Well, Johnnie, how are you?"

The aged celestial, not understanding a word though comprehending the roughness, remained silent, whereon the European exclaimed insolently, "Who are you staring at, you old fool?"

At this point the village dogs, excited by such an unexpected invasion, commenced to bark, and were instantly stoned by the intruders, so that the old Chinaman, to avoid being struck, hurried into his house and closed the door, while the sportsmen and their troop passed through the sleepy hamlet like a whirlwind, scaring women, children, fowls and pigs and disgusting the inhabitants by their uncouthness. Such behaviour, I fear, is only too common.

In my experience it is seldom that a courteous bearing does not meet with immediate friendly response.

As the wind was dropping and there were signs of rain I left my new-made friends and returned to the little bay beneath the cliffs, where we had spent the previous night. Before dark the rain was coming down steadily, but having rigged tarpaulins over the hood and awning we so far kept dry and comfortable.

In the middle of the night I was awakened by a torrential downpour and by the roar of a heavy gale as it swept over the cliffs high above our heads. Despite the tarpaulins the wet found its way in and soaked us to the skin, so that with daylight we were glad to make preparations for returning to Kiukiang.

The awning we took in, but the lashings of the tarpaulins which covered the hood were so tightened by moisture that it was impossible to unknot them, and so the structure was left standing.

Starting off under the jib alone with the wind dead astern, it was not until the shelter of the cliffs had been left and return was already impossible that I realised what we were in for.

The gale was a perfect hurricane, before which we flew at a tremendous pace. The further we left the land the higher the swell became, until it suddenly dawned on me that our chances of covering the four or five miles before reaching the creek were not very bright.

I have not been in many tight places, but this certainly was one.

The boatmen had realised our dangerous straits, and failing at the pinch, as I have seen Chinamen do before and since, crouched down with faces blanched to putty and almost too terror-stricken to bail out the water which we shipped in ever-increasing quantities.

A thick mist of driven spray covered the surface of the lake, and the boat rolled wildly in the waves, which although not very high were short and heavy and hissed as if in a rapid.

We should have been swamped over the stern again and again had it not been for the hood, which more by good fortune than by design I had left standing. The tiller happily was a long one, and by exerting all my strength we kept a fairly straight course, eventually dashing through clouds of driven foam into the creek, though in a half-swamped condition. We had got off scot-free, but it had been touch and go. If the hood and tarpaulins had failed to keep out the seas we should have been pooped, and if the jib-sheets had carried away or the rudder become unshipped we should have broached to, when immediate destruction would have been our lot.

The remainder of the journey was simple enough, and in a few hours we were safely back in port.

Both at Hongkong and Shanghai, where the European population numbers several thousands, there is a yacht club, each containing several up-to-date classes, ranging from half-raters to fifteen-tonners, and regattas under various conditions are of frequent occurrence. These clubs, as well as the yachts, being practically identical with those in this country, it is unnecessary to enter into details.

At Hongkong the sailing is on a bright, blue sea, whether in the magnificent harbour or amongst the numerous lovely islands, while at Shanghai it is on the muddy waters of the Whangpoo, which, except for the fact that it is the harbour of this thriving settlement, where scores of vessels of all sizes and nationalities ride at anchor or are berthed alongside wharves, is a small and uninteresting river flowing into the estuary of the Yangtse.

From the ancient Portuguese colony of Macao, distant forty miles from Hongkong and celebrated as the home of the poet Camoes, come fleets of fishing-boats, which, in pursuit of their calling, cruise amongst the islands in the delta of the West River.

These "Macao junks" are about the best sea-boats and the fastest sailers of all Chinese vessels.

Built on graceful lines, and of light material, they possess the buoyancy of a duck, rarely shipping water even in the heaviest sea, while with two masts carrying well-shaped sails of matting, immense perforated, balanced rudders, and being of light draught, they handle so well that they can turn a complete circle in their own length. While unable to sail as close to the wind as a yacht, their chief point is in running, when with huge sails set on either side they will tear along at a pace perfectly astounding for craft of their unpretentious build and rig.

During a pleasant two years' sojourn in this colony I sailed a smart little cutter of about one and a half tons, so that I was able to thoroughly test the merits of these junks, and while rather more than holding my own on all points in a light breeze, I could only make a good show in strong winds and rough water when sailing full and by, and was considerably outpaced in running free.

Although these waters are infested with pirates and smugglers, as evidenced by such names as "Dead Man's Grave," "Robbers' Point," "Grave Island," "Pirates' Creek" and the like, Europeans are but seldom molested, and although generally taking my Winchester as a precautionary measure when going any distance from port, I have spent many delightful days in standing out to sea, sailing through the numerous creeks with which the hinterland is intersected, or in cruising amongst the islands, on which sometimes I would land, and creeping round the rocky shores with my gun would frequently surprise wildfowl feeding amongst the shallow bays and pools.

At other times, in company with a convivial friend, I would get under way in the cool of the evening, and after running out to sea for an hour or so to enjoy the night breezes setting in from the Pacific, and perhaps laying to for a swim, we would return to the lovely bay, and dropping anchor off the Praia Grande dine by moonlight to the strains of the Portuguese military band, which played two or three times weekly either at the Governor's Palace or in the public gardens, both of which overlooked the sea.

When on a trip up the Sikiang or West River from Canton to Wuchow, I observed many junks fitted with what may be described as an adjustable cut-water or bow-board.

These vessels, having great beam and perfectly flat bottoms, would only draw a few inches, and as their provenance was evidently from shallow waters, where neither keels, centre-boards nor lee-boards could be employed, recourse was had to enormous rudders and these cut-waters as a means of hauling a wind, the device apparently answering fairly well.

As far as I could see, a deep groove was cut along the stem, and the bow-board, perhaps three feet in width, was slipped into it and made fast at the top with a lashing.

In beating to windward these cut-waters were in position, but when running free they were unshipped and laid on the foredeck.

Wherever foreigners congregate, but more especially at Shanghai and up the Yangtse, the house-boat, combining comfort, convenience and fair sailing powers, is a favourite means of getting about on shooting trips and picnics, and altogether forms an important feature of the pleasant existence which we lead in the Far East.

The hull usually resembles that of a light-draught yacht, with either a drop-keel or lee-boards, so that shallow creeks may be readily entered.

In rig they are semi-Chinese, the shape of the sail being that of the ordinary balanced lug, which bamboo reefing battens with a sheet-line leading from the extremity of each to the main-sheet render extremely handy and safe. A jib can also be set, but as it destroys the simplicity of the rig it is greatly disliked by the crew and therefore seldom utilised.

The particular craft which I have now in mind is an excellent sea-boat, fast and comfortable, has a fine cabin with four berths, tables folding on either side of the centre-board well, and capable of seating a dozen, stove, gun-racks, glass and bottle brackets and numerous lockers. There is also a bathroom and lavatory, a kitchen with good cooking range, quarters forrard for the crew--which consists of the lowdah and four sailors, together with cook, boy and dog-coolie--while on deck are the water-tanks, kennels, and a small sampan by way of a jolly.

Replete with every comfort, a shooting-box for the sportsman and a sure refuge for the overworked, the house-boat represents to me the acme of leisure and repose.

"And the night shall be fill'd with music, And the cares that infest the day Shall fold their tents like the Arabs, And as silently steal away."

CHAPTER VI

JAMBOREES

It is nearing twenty years ago since I celebrated my last bump supper in my old college at Cambridge, but the remembrance of it is so bright and cheering in the monotony of daily life that time is much abridged, and it seems but yesterday that the two pailfuls of smoking milk punch worked such deadly havoc amongst four crews of well-trained men that ultimately they were mostly laid out in a row, with consequent sore heads and interviews with the dean next morning. A bump supper is an orgy never to be forgotten.

A jamboree is a very analogous function. Where and what the word comes from I do not know, but its meaning in the Far East is universally understood to be a bachelor entertainment consisting of an enormous dinner with plenty of wine, tales, songs and general hilarity, occasionally verging on riotousness with breakage of household furniture and other effects.

As I glance back over the past fifteen years such wild nights stand out like beacons in pleasing relief from the many respectable gatherings, be it in Church or Society, at which I have had the honour of assisting, but which have left no impressions sufficiently vivid to class them with treasured souvenirs or even provoke a smile.

Some years since there visited Hankow a personage of exalted rank, who, being a near kinsman of one of the most powerful of Europe's present rulers, was received with patriotic enthusiasm by the large colony of his nationals domiciled there, and with every mark of respect by all other members of the cosmopolitan community.

His arrival in one of the fine Chinese river-boats was signalised by what might have been a fatal catastrophe but for the skilful manoeuvring of his ship by the veteran American skipper.

Just as the vessel had threaded her way through numerous ocean steamers and foreign gun-boats anchored in the stream, and was slowly approaching the hulk alongside which she was to be made fast, an enormous raft of timber, bearing a whole village of huts and a considerable population of raft navigators, caught by the swirling eddy caused by a freshet from the River Han, which 200 yards above this point was pouring at right angles into the mighty Yangtse's five-knot current, bore swiftly down on the steamer, threatening to strike her amidships and either pin her to the hulk or crush her against the stone-faced bund, when she must have been immediately sunk. Unaware of the danger until it was almost upon him, the captain had just time to reverse his engines, and by going full speed astern with the helm hard over bring his ship round so as to receive the threatened blow end on instead of abeam. The impact nearly drove the vessel's stern into the hulk, but with her engines now going full speed ahead, and churning up two white lanes of foam with her paddle-wheels, she rammed her bows into the raft, and just managing to deflect its course they floated down with the stream locked together, until by a miracle they had passed clear of all the shipping, though at times only by a few feet, and the steamer with her illustrious passenger again bore up for her berth, after the narrowest of escapes but without having sustained the slightest damage.

These enormous rafts, composed chiefly of bamboos and pines, generally come from the forests of Hunan, and after crossing the Tongting lake float down the Yangtse to places where wood is scarce and a good market obtains. They vary in size, but sometimes are a hundred yards in length by twenty in breadth, and draw probably from ten to twenty feet. With their huts of bamboo and matting, with long sweeps both ahead and astern for steering, and great coils of plaited bamboo ropes for mooring purposes, they present an extremely picturesque appearance.

Amongst other festivities arranged by his compatriots in honour of the distinguished visitor, a banquet, preceded by a reception of prominent residents, was given at the club. It being almost midsummer, the weather was fearfully hot, the thermometer registering over ninety after sundown, and as a notification had been issued with all invitations that black evening dress would be de rigueur we were debarred from wearing our cool, white mess jackets, and all arrived at the club almost melting inside thick broadcloths.

A very amusing little episode occurred at the reception.

Amongst the few ladies present were the wife and daughter of a Western official. They had evidently been "raised" away from the beaten tracks of Society and crowned heads had not been their daily companions. On this party being presented, the official and his wife preserved a diplomatic silence, but mademoiselle was not inclined to take things for granted, and seeing neither golden crown nor purple robe she evidently had misgivings. "Are you really the grand duke?" she inquired with striking accent; "are you really a prince?" The prince smilingly replied that such was the case, on which his fair interrogator exclaimed, "Oh, my! I am surprised," and then slowly retired from the front but with many backward glances of unconcealed disappointment.

A large number of residents had received the honour of an invitation, probably a hundred sitting down, and, as is customary in China, each guest brought his own servant, so that from a hundred and fifty to two hundred people were assembled in one large room, which together with the hot dishes and a great many lamps caused the temperature to go up several degrees, adding greatly to the discomfort we already experienced owing to our thick clothes.

To still further increase the torture, a crowd of Chinese which had collected in the streets below commenced to throw stones through the open windows. One passed between my right-hand neighbour and myself, shivering my wine-glasses to atoms. The windows and shutters were hastily closed, and very shortly the temperature must have still further increased by several degrees. Champagne flowed in streams, a short speech of welcome was made by the local sport, to which the guest of honour replied, "White Wings" was sung by the doctor, and the parboiled throng descended to the lower precincts of the building to watch a display of fireworks. The heat was awful. Not a breath of air, and the sulphurous smoke from the fireworks hung low on the ground in white masses, and seemed to seek shelter in the club, for in a very short time the place was flooded with the choking fumes which caused one to feel a tightness across the chest and a stinging in the eyes, and which made it impossible to see across the room.

The prince withdrew at a somewhat early hour, and after a time the guests commenced to disperse.

The heat, the champagne and the sulphur smoke had proved too much for me. I attempted to walk straight, but the power to do so was gone. First one foot would strike a hill, then the other would go down into a deep hole, and so on, while lamp-posts and buildings seemed to whirl past and round at a fearful pace.

When nearing my quarters I heard a faint "hillo" from a by-street, and a continental mess-mate stumbled almost into my arms. He fully intended to do so and I had no wish to avoid him but somehow we missed each other and both fell prostrate on the pavement. Far from feeling any ill-humour at this catastrophe, we both thought it a capital joke, and I can distinctly remember our sitting side by side in the gutter and swearing eternal friendship. After this things are vague, and the next I remember is going upstairs on all fours and then opening my bedroom door. A most remarkable sight presented itself. I have seen mirage in the Arabian desert, but I have never seen anything like that. There was my bed, shrunk to the size of about one inch in length, at the top corner of the room near the ceiling, dancing up and down at the end of a bright and circling tunnel. How to get there I did not know. I can just remember sinking on hands and knees in order to attempt the climb, when the floor struck me so violently in the face that I lost consciousness, awaking late next morning to find myself reclining on the bed, but still in my dress clothes. My friend, it was said, attempted to go to bed in his bath, where he was discovered in full evening dress, scooping the water over himself and complaining that he could not keep the sheets up. But this is by the way.

At Kiukiang, where I happened to be a few years later, the community was small, consisting of a few married couples and perhaps half a dozen bachelors.

Time hung like lead, and small wonder that now and again we young men would foregather round the festive board, when high spirits long pent up would burst forth with a vim that is but rarely attained in places offering perennial sources of amusement.

On the occasion in question the dinner was at our mess, which, besides myself, consisted of an Italian and a tall American of stern and unbending nature. Our guests were two Russians and two Scotchmen, all we could muster, but excellent in quality. After a jovial repast we sallied forth on to the bund, and being a bright moonlight night, romance entered into our souls, and we started to serenade the various ladies of the port. First to the Consulate, where we drew up in line on the lawn, the time being 2 a.m., and rendered "God Save the Queen" with great execution and considerable pathos, notwithstanding pronounced differences in American, Italian, Scotch, Russian and English accentuation. Subsequently visits were made to all the other houses, with the exception of one, where we rather feared to intrude, as the good lady, while very affable as a rule, would stand no nonsense, and when she did not wish to be pleasant could treat one to a touch of sarcasm which would last for some time. However, we finally summoned up courage and approached the house as noiselessly and guiltily as a gang of thieves. The front gate was locked and eight feet high, but after some delay we scaled it, ranged ourselves on the lower verandah and were halfway through "My Bonnie Lives over the Ocean," when a crash overhead announced that we were in for a storm. I have never in my life seen seven men break and fly in such utter terror. Once off the verandah into the moonlight we were in full view of the outraged dame, who stood in a commanding attitude on the upper verandah in her dressing-gown, almost speechless with emotion, but gesticulating frantically. We rushed at the gate, and in our eagerness to be on the other side fought and wrestled with each other for first place. The upper bars broke away in our hands, bricks came off the top of the adjoining walls, and it was fully five minutes before we were in the road, breathless, with torn clothes, and I, personally, with a sprained wrist.

We now felt we were in for a bad time next day, and so, to revive our drooping spirits, repaired to the house of one of the Russians. Here vodka, caviare, salmon-back, sardines, Bologna sausage and other little dainties common to the zacousca furnished us with a most recherch?supper. We ate everything and drank a good deal. By this time we were again in the wildest spirits and fit for anything. Our tall American friend was still somewhat unbent, and being of an inquiring turn of mind was examining the trap-door through which the dinner is handed by the cook from the pantry into the dining-room. No sooner was his head well through than he was pounced on by the two Caledonians, who, seizing him by the legs below the knee, shot his six feet odd through the trap-door as if they had been tossing the caber. A terrific crash of crockery told its own tale; the Russian's best dinner service was no more. Rising from the fragments the victim declared it to be his opinion that all, with the exception of himself, were inebriated and unfit for the society of respectable citizens, after which delivery he withdrew to his own quarters.

Next we heard female shrieks and screams, accompanied by a heavy tramping of feet down the stairs, and two of our joyous band appeared, bearing in triumph by her head and her heels, the struggling form of our host's Chinese housekeeper, clad in nothing but her night garments. She was laid tenderly on the dining-room table and comforted with some Veuve Clicquot champagne, for the poor creature had been somewhat upset by being pounced on when asleep in bed and hauled off with so little ceremony and preparation into the publicity of a well-lighted room full of masculine visitors.

Shortly after daylight the company separated with many expressions of mutual esteem. On my way to bed I thought our American chum should be interviewed and an explanation made that no offence was intended by the recent treatment of him. He was in bed and sleeping heavily, so I was obliged to wake him in order to fulfil my mission of peace. To say that he received these overtures in a friendly spirit would be incorrect. He seemed to be preparing for immediate hostilities, and so, not to be taken at a disadvantage, I closed with him as he leaped out of bed. The m 阮閑 lasted probably five minutes, during which brief period his furniture was hurled in chaotic profusion all round the room, my black mess jacket was divided up the back from the tail to the collar, his pyjamas carried away, and the skin was detached from his bare feet by my boots. So ended a glorious evening. Next day we all lay low, but learnt that a certain person had interviewed the Consul with a view to legal proceedings for alleged housebreaking. Our enemy, however, was check-mated, and ourselves saved, by the veracious testimony of a dear old Scotch lady, who lived in the adjoining house, and who declared that our serenade was "verra nice though a wee bit muxed," and that she herself had enjoyed it immensely.

One often hears of the flower-boats of Canton, and immediately associates them with gaily-painted gondolas, tenanted by captivating sirens and decorated with perfumed flowers and plants, growing with a luxurious profusion common only to the Flowery Land. "Flower-girl" is the universal Chinese term for those young women who dance and sing in public, and who for regular fees attend at Chinese dinner-parties, composed exclusively of men, to flirt with the guests while filling their pipes and pouring out their wine. Poor parents having larger families than they can support frequently sell one or two of their best-looking daughters to professional trainers, who, after teaching them to dance and sing, send them to the flower-boats in hopes that they may there captivate wealthy habitu 閣, when handsome prices would be realised.

These girls are frequently not of bad character, but being on the marriage market employ their wiles to secure husbands, in which they sometimes succeed, passing into the hands of rich Chinese for three, four or five hundred dollars, according to their merits, as wives of an inferior rank, say number four or six.

At various places in the south, but especially at Canton and Wuchow, a number of large, ugly junks with spacious cabins are moored alongside each other in a certain locality. They possess no very striking features, and those I have seen at Wuchow were absolutely devoid of flowers or plants of any kind, the name "flower-boat" signifying nothing more than the haunt of the flower-girl.

In the cabins of these craft it is the fashionable thing amongst well-to-do Chinamen to hold their jamborees. They hire a particular junk for a certain date, and at the appointed hour the party assembles there, being received by two or three unprepossessing servants. Dinner, or whatever form the entertainment may take, is commenced, and as general mirth rises with the good cheer, guests write on a slate provided for the purpose the names of such flower-girls as they may fancy. This slate is quickly carried to where the girls live, hard by, and shortly they will appear, staying for a time to dance, sing and dally with their admirers, after which they will pass on to other boats to fulfil further engagements.

The singing is execrable, being a high, nasal falsetto, and the dancing, or rather swaying on their tiny feet while waving overhead a dirty cloth in their beautifully-shaped hands, is feeble in the extreme. A band of musicians is usually engaged, after protracted haggling, to enliven the proceedings. Two or three native fiddles of most primitive make wail incessantly, cymbals clash recklessly, a kind of flute resembling bagpipes in sound squirls, while a wooden drum adds to the deafening din. The girls squeak and posture, the place reeks with pungent tobacco smoke and the smell of garlic, the guests munch dried melon seeds, spitting the husks on to the floor, and shout to make each other hear above the general uproar.

To escape from this inferno was the chief pleasure of the evening, and any romantic ideas I may have had with respect to "flower-boats" will remain shattered for ever.

Macao has been a Portuguese colony for upwards of three centuries, it having been ceded to its original settlers by the viceroy of Canton in recognition of services rendered by those intrepid buccaneers in freeing neighbouring waters from pirates and robbers. It is a most quaint and interesting little place, wearing a look of medi 鑿 al times, and still possessing many traces of former prosperity, though now chiefly remarkable for its legalised gambling facilities, for which reason it is frequently called the Monte Carlo of the Far East, there being also a certain natural resemblance.

At Hongkong gambling is strictly prohibited amongst the Chinese, while at Canton gaming-houses are heavily taxed, so that natives come in great numbers from both places to Macao in order to play fantan without constant dread of police interference. All fantan shops, as they are called, contain but one gambling-table each, which is on the ground floor. This table is covered with a fine grass mat and surrounded on three sides with benches for the players, while on the fourth side sit the croupier and the banker or shroff. In the ceiling a large hole has been cut immediately over, and corresponding in size with, the table, and a railing placed round it in the room above, so that players can mount to the first floor, and bending over the railing look directly down on the gambling. In the centre of the table lies a thin slab of lead about six inches square, the sides of which represent the numbers one, two, three and four.

The croupier has immediately in front of him a pile of bright copper cash, perhaps two pints. From these he takes a large double-handful, which he places well on the table and covers with a small metal bowl. Now is the time for making bets on the four numbers. Suppose we put a dollar on number three. In the course of a few minutes all those who desire to bet have done so, stakes from the first floor being put into a basket by an attendant and lowered on to the table by means of a string, and the little square of lead is surrounded with coins, notes and counters arranged by the shroff. Now the croupier, with a thin stick about a foot in length, commences to scrape away four coins at a time from the double-handful of cash. One, two, three, four. One, two, three, four, and so on. The little heap begins to diminish. The eager gamblers, who are generally all Chinese, bend forward with straining eyes to within a few inches of the croupier's stick, so that any cheating would be well-nigh impossible. One, two, three, four. Only a few more cash. The excitement is intense. One, two, three.... Three cash remain!

Number three wins. All those who bet on one, two and four lose their stakes, while those who bet on three receive five times the amount of their stakes after a deduction of twenty-five per cent. has been made. We put a dollar on number three; well, after deducting twenty-five per cent. from it as profit for the table, seventy-five cents are left, and we receive five times that amount, which is equal to three dollars and seventy-five cents.

These fantan shops, of which there may be twenty or thirty, are all licensed and kept under strict supervision, being farmed out to rich syndicates by the Portuguese authorities, the large sums thus realised forming no inconsiderable part of the colony's revenue.

Play goes on day and night all the year round, Sundays included, and is practically unlimited, for it is possible to bet from five cents to five hundred dollars at a time. Large sums are continually won and lost, it being a common thing to see gamblers, both men and women, after staking their last cash hand over watches, jewellery and other valuables to the shroff for valuation, and hazard all on a final throw to retrieve their losses.

This standing temptation of the fantan shops is a fertile source of crime, especially amongst domestic servants, for apart from the Chinaman's inborn love of gambling, in the event of their being in financial straits, as is frequently the case, a possible way out of such difficulties is by stealthily taking certain objects from their master's house, say a clock and a dozen silver spoons, pledging them at one of the numerous pawn-shops and gambling with the proceeds. If fortune be favourable the clock and spoons are immediately redeemed and returned before being missed, while the servant has found an easy way out of his difficulties. On the other hand, should luck be against the player, he either bolts to another part of the country or brazens out the theft by declaring that the house has been broken into by burglars.

Trusted servants who have been many years in one employ frequently yield to this alluring but hazardous appeal to chance.

One morning as I was leaving Macao for Hongkong by the daily steamer a Chinese passenger suddenly leaped overboard. The ship was stopped and a boat quickly lowered, while a Portuguese police launch also dashed to the rescue, but although we could see the suicide's head above water for some time he sank before help arrived. Having ruined himself at fantan he dared not return to Hongkong.

And such is the fate of many.

A Chinese banquet is a weird festivity, and once gone through will never be forgotten.

On the occasion which I will attempt to describe invitations were issued for 10 a.m., but in accordance with celestial custom the guests did not arrive till about 11.30, when, after waiting half an hour, during which the company chatted, drank tea and smoked, we were ushered into a large hall with brick floor and paper windows, where the repast was spread on three round tables, at each of which were three Europeans and five or six Chinese, our hosts, clad in their beautiful silk official robes, while we wore black morning coats.

The tables were of plain wood and without table-cloths, while the luxuriously-cushioned divans of Far East imaginings were hard wooden stools.

Numbers of little dishes containing dried fruits, sweets, pickles, slices of ham, preserved eggs (more than a year old, black and highly offensive), vegetables, etc., loaded the festive boards.

Each feaster was provided with a pair of chopsticks and two small sheets of brown paper with which to wipe them after each course.

Warm yellow wine of a peculiar musty flavour and sadly lacking in potency, was poured by attendants from pewter kettles into small wine-cups, to be tossed off in bumpers all round with great frequency, each guest immediately presenting his empty cup to the gaze of his neighbours to show that there had been no heel-taps. It looked as though we were simultaneously levelling revolvers at each other's heads.

At a given signal the fray began. All the Chinese rose up, took their chopsticks, and plunging them into various dishes began helping us, the guests of honour. On my one small plate were quickly deposited some sweets, sour pickles, dried fruit, slices of ham, and one of the notorious eggs.

Now we in turn were expected to rise up and return the compliment by helping our helpers. I clutched my sticks, drove them into a piece of fish and dropped it into my neighbour's wine. Tableau! Never mind, I tried pickles and preserves in detail with about an average success. No good came of my efforts, but neither did any harm, for our entertainers smiled and bowed and rose from their seats in gracious acknowledgment of our strenuous but futile attempts to do the correct thing.

All this was but a preliminary canter taking the place of our dessert, albeit coming before the meal instead of at the end.

Hot courses were now placed on the table, our Chinese friends helping us from them with their chopsticks, which they manipulated with marvellous dexterity.

1. Puddings of several kinds Too sweet. 2. Fresh-water Fish (boiled) Insipid. 3. Chickens (boiled) Fair. 4. Sea Slugs Passed. 5. Shrimps Nasty. 6. White Mushrooms Good. 7. Eels First-rate. 8. Sea-weed Tough as leather. 9. White Bait Good. 10. Interiors of Fish Good heavens!!! 11. Lotus Nuts and Milk Very good. 12. Chicken (boiled in different manner) Passed. 13. Rissoles of Frogs Je ne sais pas. 14. Pork and Rice Flour A curious mixture. 15. Sugared Rice Too sweet. 16. Duck (boiled) Excellent, the best dish. 17. Shark's Fins Very good. 18. Porridge No thanks. 19. Soup Passed. 20. Opium, cigars, etc. On this occasion opium was not smoked.

This long menu was gone through accompanied with an abundance of talk, compliments, jokes and the emission of various sounds peculiar to the Chinese while feeding.

Immediately on rising from table we donned our hats, saluted ?la Chinoise by shaking our clasped hands in each other's faces, "Nin ching. Poo sung, poo sung," and took our departure, bowing repeatedly and walking backwards.

CHAPTER VII

AROUND PEKING

The translation of the word Peking is "capital of the North," and is so called in contradistinction to Nanking[1] or "capital of the South."

Peking is not a Chinese city at all, although generally supposed to be so, but a Tartar city, which, instead of the jumble of narrow, paved streets habitually found in all Chinese towns, was originally designed and laid out on a plan probably excelling in grandeur that of any other city in the world. That the result, as seen in the city of to-day, is but a mockery of the magnificent idea which possessed the master mind that conceived it, is due to that trait of the Mongolian temperament which exhausts itself in the conception and completion of some gigantic undertaking, leaving it thenceforth to moulder and decay, until in succeeding ages it stands gaunt witness of human wisdom, folly and neglect. Such are Peking, the Great Wall and the Grand Canal.

Although adjoining the Tartar, there is a Chinese city, it is so squalid and of such mean pretensions that with the exception of a single street it is of but little interest to Europeans, so that when speaking of Peking it is the Tartar city alone that one has in mind.

Surrounded by an immense rectangular wall, some sixty feet in height, with a width of twenty feet at the top and forty feet at the base, and pierced at regular intervals by picturesque and towering gateways, between which wide boulevards traverse the city from end to end and from side to side, but which, instead of being paved and lighted, are but lanes of filth, ankle deep in dust during dry weather, to be quickly changed by rain into rivers of black mud, continuously churned up by the wheels of springless carts, and spattered far and wide by the plunging feet of straining quadrupeds.

On either side of, and frequently several feet below, these highways are mud paths, along which pedestrians wend a varied way, avoiding cesspools, stepping over transverse timbers or circumventing squatters' huts, showered on the while by splashings from the highroad or blinded by clouds of refuse-laden dust.

The only attempt at lighting is by means of lanterns, which, with heavy wooden frames covered with paper instead of glass and placed at intervals of perhaps a quarter of a mile, throw out rays to the extent of one candle-power each.

From the streets very few buildings of any pretensions can be discerned, while from the dominating eminence of the city wall a sea of roofs monotonous in equality of height and greyness of colour meets the eye, which sameness is mostly due to the facts that but few upper storeys exist, and that the residences of the wealthy, besides being screened by high outer walls, are so blended with shops and hovels that it is difficult to discriminate them.

In the heart of Peking, and surrounded by a twenty-foot wall coped with tiles glazed yellow and green, is the forbidden city, where the imperial palaces are grouped and from which Europeans were until recently jealously excluded.

The city walls; a few temples in varying stages of magnificence, tawdriness and decay; the remains of sewers which, built of solid blocks of stone and large enough to admit a donkey, show that formerly a scheme of drainage and sanitation existed although to-day there is nothing of the kind; an insignificant canal and a hill rumoured to be made of coal heaped there as a supply in case of siege; and one has seen the architectural wonders of the capital.

"Legation Quarter" prior to the Boxer troubles was but an indefinite area of the city in which the legations "happened" from time to time amongst a squalid entourage of native buildings, and connected one with another by means of impossible thoroughfares which passed for streets.

A Russian diplomat once said to me that he considered Peking "dirty but nice," and this description exactly coincides with my own idea. This wasted body on a majestic frame carries one back with a single step to civilisation of a thousand years ago. Not the remnants displayed to tourists in Greece or Rome but the real thing, over which the Western spirit of change has as yet worked but little alteration.

In this vast museum of antiquities one finds at every turn objects of engrossing interest, and personally it seemed to me that many of the scenes depicted in Prescott's enchanting book, The Conquest of Mexico, might almost as well have been laid in this far-famed capital of the North. Great antiquity, isolation from the Western world, pride of race and empire, veneration for their own colossal literature, arrested civilisation and profound contempt for all things foreign, create a picture rich in detail, very mournful in subject and marvellous in perspective.

The means of getting about are by cart, on horseback or afoot, the sedan chair, which in other places furnishes the most comfortable conveyance, being here reserved for members of the Imperial family and for high officials both native and foreign.

The carts, which ply for hire like cabs, are massive, springless tumbrils covered with a wain. In fine weather the passenger, with a view to less discomfort, usually sits on the splashboard with his back rubbing against the hind-quarters of the pony or mule and his feet dangling in front of the wheel, which plays on to them a continuous stream of dirt and dust. In windy weather one must crawl inside and sit on the floor tailor fashion, there being no seat, and then let down the curtain, thus effectually blocking all view but keeping out most of the dust, which, flying in blinding clouds, would quickly reduce one to a state of absolute filth, filling the clothes, hair, ears and mouth and guttering down from the nose and eyes. To this foul dust is due the terrible amount of ophthalmia and consequent blindness so prevalent throughout the East.

In rainy weather carts sink up to the axle in black liquid mud, which flies in all directions from the wheels, and at each footfall of horse or mule, splattering pedestrians and shop-fronts on the sidewalks and smothering other vehicles as they pass.

To such an indescribable state are the streets reduced by heavy rains that I actually remember a mule being drowned in the shafts by the side of one of the main thoroughfares in the very heart of the city.

Luckily for all concerned there is a large percentage of beautiful weather, when mud and dust alike are absent and when one can canter noiselessly along the soft, yielding roads, which are then in much the same condition for riding as is Rotten Row.

On such mornings as these Peking is delightful, with its bright sun, cool, bracing air and interesting sights, while through the cloudless sky flocks of pigeons, having whistles of wood or clay fastened to their feet and tails, make strange yet pleasing sounds varied with every twist and turn of flight.

A noticeable trait of Chinese character, and one fostered, if not generated, by Buddhistic teaching, is an undemonstrative fondness for animals, or, I might rather say, a passive admission of their right to considerate treatment, and strangely enough animals, both wild and domesticated, appear to comprehend this sentiment, for while greatly scared at the approach of a European they usually take but little heed of the presence of Chinese.

It is a common thing to see a well-dressed Chinaman sauntering along holding up a bent stick to which a bird is attached by a string some four feet or so in length, so that the little prisoner can make short flights to the limit of its tether and return again to its perch, gaily chirping and singing the while.

Another stroller will be carrying a wicker bird-cage on the hand, bent back and upraised to the shoulder, much as a waiter carries dishes, containing generally a Tientsin lark or other celebrated songster, and on arriving at some open spot will place the cage on the ground, and retiring to a short distance whistle to the bird, which will shortly burst into song, to the evident delight of both owner and bystanders.

Outside one of the gateways is a kind of bazaar, which we foreigners generally called "Bird-cage walk," for there the bird-fanciers lived, and birds of many different kinds were exposed for sale, not in cages, but quite tame, and quietly sitting on perches--parrots, larks, Java sparrows, etc., some of them tied by the leg, but not all.

Here, too, were to be seen wicker baskets, much resembling orange crates, full of common sparrows, representing a regular supply for a regular demand. Benevolent old Chinamen, fl 鈔 eurs and literati would visit this bazaar of an afternoon with the sole object of buying a few of these little birds for two or three cash each and then letting them fly away, a beatific smile betraying the salve to inward feelings generated by a knowledge of merit acquired, any miseries inflicted on the sparrows by capture and confinement counting for nothing in the balance against the good work accomplished by their purchase and release.

The Chinese ideas of life and death are very dissimilar to our own.

With us, the responsibility of parents for the bringing up and well-being of the children is paramount, the fulfilment of such obligations being enforced both by legal and social pressure, while the responsibility of children for the care of their aged parents is almost nil.

Amongst the Chinese, children are considered to be the absolute chattels of the parents, with whose treatment of their offspring neither public opinion nor the country's laws have any right of interference. Infanticide can be, and undoubtedly is to a certain extent, practised, while the father is even said to be legally entitled to punish his grown-up children with death.

Children, on the other hand, are bound by every tie to obey, respect, support and even worship the authors of their being. Filial duty is the greatest of all virtues, and the man who fails in this respect is despised by everyone and takes rank with worthless characters and outcasts.

Our view of life is very finite. We are born, we die, are relegated to the unknown and quickly forgotten.

A Chinaman regards himself as a disseverable part of the stream of life, by which he is borne into this world to live his life here, and then is borne on again to the abode of departed spirits without continuity of existence having been interrupted. At his death he is mourned with a whole-hearted sincerity by his entire family, who perform the obsequies with great respect and as much display as is compatible with their station in life. An imposing grave is built in a spot facing a pleasant prospect, while trees are planted, and sometimes even artificial pieces of water made, so that the disembodied spirit may be able to enjoy shady groves and cooling breezes. Sacrifices are offered at this shrine not once, but year after year, and by his children's children, with an absolute certainty of the spirit's existence and approving knowledge. This is the practice of ancestral worship, and greatly to be pitied is the man who leaves no son to perform sacrifices at his grave.

In Peking funeral processions assume gigantic proportions.

I have seen them more than a mile in length, and of such barbaric magnificence that they must have cost many thousands of ounces of silver.

Life-sized horses, camels, ostriches and other animals made of cardboard or cotton wool, houses of lath and paper, as well as strings of imitation gold and silver money to be burnt at the grave and so wafted to the next world for use of the departed spirit, tablets embossed with golden Chinese characters, and lanterns of varied size and shape are carried in advance by an army of riffraff. A band of priests chanting, or playing weird dirges on instruments much resembling bagpipes in sound, immediately precedes the catafalque, an immense edifice from ten to fifteen feet in height, containing the coffin and covered with beautiful hangings of embroidered silk, and which is carried bodily on massive red poles some nine inches in diameter, by as many as forty or fifty bearers. Mourners with dishevelled hair and clothed in long white gowns follow on foot, in carts or in chairs, according to the rank held by the deceased.

Winter in Northern China is extremely severe, and Tientsin, the port of Peking, is yearly closed to navigation for six or eight weeks through the sea and river being frozen. The thermometer frequently falls below zero, but owing to a bright atmosphere the cold is not felt so much as might be expected. At night the stars blink and blaze with intense brilliancy, and the still, frosty air seems almost to ring with a metallic voice. Beggars and homeless wanderers are nightly frozen by the dozen, and the whole land lies powerless in the grip of King Frost.

My bedroom I could keep fairly warm by means of a large American stove heated up till it was white, but in the mornings, on passing into my bathroom, which boasted a brick floor and paper windows, I found the temperature almost coinciding with that of the open air, albeit a small stove roared in the corner, while steam from the hot water in a wooden bath was so thick as to make the daylight dim. Ablutions were a hurried function, ending in precipitate retreat to the warmth of the bedroom. The small stove would burn itself out, the steam would congeal and disappear, and the bath water, unless removed, would be quickly frozen.

As winter wore on the sides of my bath-tub became coated with ice, which increased with every splash until there was a thickness of three or four inches, for it would have injured the bath to keep breaking it off, so that, ultimately, I took my morning tub in a nest of ice, only the bottom of which was completely thawed by the daily supply of hot water.

Along the streets, well-to-do Chinese appear swelled to double their usual proportions by furs and successive layers of wadded clothes, which are of such thickness as to hold the arms propped out at almost right angles to the bodies, while their heads are enveloped in bright-coloured hoods buttoning tight under the chin. Poor, half-naked beggars, clasping their rice-bowls and bent double by the cold, shamble along, muttering and moaning, while their starving, rolling eyes scan the faces of passers-by in mute appeal for help or pity.

One evening, as I was riding along one of the principal streets, I saw a

Chinaman carrying home a hot, steaming cake, something like a Yorkshire pudding with raisins in it, which he had just bought at a wayside cook-shop, when a beggar suddenly seized him by both wrists, and taking as large a mouthful as he could bite out of the pastry, shuffled off, heedless of the blows rained on him by the irate purchaser.

On the coldest days I have seen beggars collected in groups and gambling for the few cash they possessed, the total sum probably not exceeding a halfpenny. Naked, hungry and frozen, they watched with tense features and straining eyes the fatal issue of their throw for either a meal or death that night by cold and starvation.

Accustomed to want and misery, they appear pleased with any trifle that may fall into their hands, and on a bitter, windy day I have seen grown-up beggars on a waste patch flying a kite and enjoying the pastime with a gusto denied to more blas?pursuers of this aerial sport.

Ice in Northern China is seldom good, as owing to the frequent winds it is generally covered with dust, although occasionally at the beginning of winter it is possible to get some fair skating before the first dust-storm.

At Peking an enormous mat shed is erected to keep out the dust, while the ground inside is flooded daily so as to secure good ice. This rink is a favourite afternoon resort of the European community, but the space is too limited and the attendance too crowded to admit of any really enjoyable skating by the light of a few oil lamps.

I have skated on the moat outside the city wall but it was not very good, the chief attraction being to watch Chinese performers. As a rule they wear only one skate, on which they propel themselves by striking the ice with the other foot until a certain speed has been attained, when they spread out their arms, bend forward until their noses almost touch the ice and raise the skateless foot high over their backs. This bird-like skim on one leg seems to be their ideal of graceful skating.

At this season the stately, two-humped camels, with beautiful coats of brown wool a foot in length, come down from Mongolia, bearing loads of meat and furs, together with frozen game and fish from Manchuria and the

Amoor river, and coal from the mines north of Peking.

The Mongol teamster, clad in skins with the hair inside, trudges in front, leading the first camel by a string attached to its nose, while a cord tied to its tail links it with the nose of the second camel, and so on, till the whole team of eight or ten are securely connected. They move along with graceful, easy stride, the only sound being the dull clanking of a heavy bell suspended from the leader's neck.

On one of the animals the Mongol's whole family is sometimes carried in two immense panniers, and the round, yellow faces of tiny children peer down from their lofty nursery on a strange and passing world.

I have also seen a calf camel, evidently cast by the way, being carried in a litter strapped to the back of its dam.

It has been told me by reliable Chinese that in winter upwards of ten thousand camels daily pass in and out of the gates of Peking. They are beautiful animals, of great height, and appear to be very meek and docile.

On one occasion, when returning at daylight from duck shooting near Marco Polo's bridge, I was tightly wedged in by several hundreds which were waiting to enter the western gateway. They looked down at me with their patient eyes as I shouted and prodded them with my whip in order to clear a way for my pony, but attempted neither to bite nor kick.

In spring their wool peels off in large flakes, giving them a ragged appearance, and is collected and woven into the celebrated Tientsin rugs.

In summer, like the wildfowl, they disappear and go north to seek cool pastures in the Mongolian highlands.

Peking not being a seaport, and as yet but little influenced by foreign trade, the European community settled there is solely composed of the corps diplomatique and the legation guards, of the inspectorate of maritime customs, of professors of the various colleges, of missionaries and a few storekeepers.

During winter, when communication with the outer world is a matter of considerable difficulty, Peking society, which is naturally of a highly cosmopolitan order, amuses itself by a constant round of dinners, balls and receptions carried out with lavish hospitality, and to which the novelty of Oriental surroundings supplies an additional attraction.

In company with a French friend, who lived in Dry Flour Alley, I made an expedition to the Great Wall, which is two days' journey from the capital.

Mounted on ponies, with provisions and bedding packed into a cart drawn by two mules, we started while it was yet dark on a cold winter's morning.

Slowly making our way along frozen roads outside the walls of the forbidden city, we arrived at one of the gateways by daylight and passed out of Peking, following a wide and dusty road, where we presently met streams of camels, mules, ponies, donkeys, carts and coolies, each bearing a load of some kind of produce wherewith to supply the markets of the great city.

It was early and bitterly cold, while everyone was too intent on his own business to do more than bestow a cursory glance on passers-by, so that our little caravan, freed from importuning curiosity, made good progress.

At about eleven o'clock we were scourged by a blinding dust-storm raised by a strong wind, to avoid which we were not sorry to take refuge in a wayside inn and there discuss an early tiffin. It was now discovered that the supply of bread necessary for our three days' trip had been left behind, so that we were obliged to content ourselves with native dough cakes, sticky and heavy as lead.

The room we occupied opened on to the courtyard of the inn, and being doorless, a small crowd of interested spectators quickly assembled to watch our every movement. This crowd continuing to grow until it consisted of several tens, my friend went out to expostulate with the innkeeper, but found that worthy busily engaged at the outer gate granting admission at five cash per head to all and sundry desirous of seeing the Europeans feed.

The wind having suddenly dropped and the sand-storm subsided we continued our journey, arriving by nightfall at the village of Yang Fang, where we had arranged to sleep.

It was here that I came very near to shuffling off my mortal coil.

Throughout the North of China brick beds called kangs are universal. They are built about two feet in height, are oblong in shape and hollow inside, with a small aperture at one end, while the top is covered with grass matting. During the day a charcoal fire is lighted in this aperture, the hot air from which fills the interior of the structure and gradually warms the brickwork, which retains its heat throughout the night. The fire is then allowed to die down, when a wadded quilt, a thick blanket and a pillow will be found sufficient to make a most comfortable couch.

I had not seen one of these kangs before and the method of heating it had not been explained to me, so, the cold being intense, I placed fresh fuel on the smouldering embers the last thing before turning in. How long I had been asleep I do not know before I became conscious of a frightful nightmare. I was very hot and had lost all power to move. My tongue felt swollen and heavy, and my throat so dry and sore that when I tried to cry out it refused to utter a sound. My eyes were smarting, and having once opened them they would not close again. My senses were clear and I knew that I was being asphyxiated, but was powerless to help myself. Horror-stricken, I watched the bright moonlight shining on the paper window until I lost consciousness.

The next thing I remember was cold air beating on my face, water in my mouth and trickling down my neck and chest, strong arms supporting me and the voice of my friend's mafoo calling to his master for a light, the moon having set.

I owed deliverance to the fortunate breaking of my pony's halter, as, having been freshly clipped, he had become restive from the cold, thereby causing the mafoo to enter my room for a spare one, which I always carried with me. The following morning I felt very shaky and had a splitting headache, but was able to continue the journey, gradually recovering as the day wore on.

It is perhaps needless to add that putting fresh charcoal on the fire was the cause of this contretemps, but I was then unaware of there being no flue to carry off the fumes.

Leaving our ponies and the cart at Yang Fang, and mounted on mules as being more surefooted, though the high wooden saddles and short stirrups were most uncomfortable, we started betimes.

After crossing a plain about ten miles in width, strewn with rocks and boulders, we reached Nan K'ow, or Southern Pass, where we entered the mountains.

The road was fairly good for pack-animals, although crossed at frequent intervals by the beds of partially-frozen streams, the swift-flowing waters of which were sweet and clear as crystal. Mountains shut us in on either side, while we met an unending procession of men and beasts conveying loads of merchandise from Mongolia to Peking.

The scenery was lovely, and all along the route were to be seen crumbling forts and walls built many centuries ago to defend this, the principal pass, against invading enemies.

We saw three or four pheasants and heard several more, so that there probably is good sport to be had amongst these rugged hills. After halting for tiffin under a fine archway of Indian architecture we arrived at Pa-Ta-Ling (eight lofty peaks), where we obtained a good view of the Great Wall.

Scrambling to the top at a place where it was partly in ruins, my friend was soon busy with his camera, whilst I proceeded to investigate this world-famed structure.

My feet are rather long and it was just fourteen of them across the top, which is evenly paved with square bricks, while the height of the wall I judged to be between twenty and thirty feet. At irregular intervals there are towers, in one of which was a pile of antique carronades about two feet long, of equal size all the way down and bound round with iron hoops for additional strength. Much resembling old rain-pipes, they had not a very formidable appearance, and were probably more dangerous to those who fired them than to the enemy.

Built two hundred years before Christ, and upwards of thirteen hundred miles in length, the wall is certainly a gigantic monument, well constructed of large bricks, and here, at any rate, in good preservation and by no means whatsoever a mass of stones and rubbish as asserted by some describers.

Instead of winding along the line of least resistance it follows the sinuosities of the country, surmounting crags and delving into valleys, so that it can be seen topping height after height as it climbs the mountain range until it becomes a mere thread and finally is lost to view in the far distance. Walking along it for some little way I found that it scaled almost perpendicular cliffs, up one of which I passed, the top of the wall here taking the form of steps, while down the opposite side the descent was so steep that for greater security I made it backwards on hands and knees.

The wall was built with the object of protecting China from the inroads of wild Tartars, who came down in hordes from Manchuria, Mongolia and the steppes of Northern Asia to seek plunder in the plains.

Chinawards there is a low parapet, while stone stairs built into the middle of the wall lead from the top through doorless gateways to the ground, giving means of ingress and exit to defenders, but on the side facing towards Mongolia the wall is crowned with battlements some four and a half feet in height, affording ample protection and pierced about every five feet with loopholes and embrasures.

One of the wonders of the world, its construction lasted ten years, and at the date of completion was probably as futile to bar the advance of a resolute foe as it would be to-day vis-?vis modern artillery.

Wishing to secure a suitable souvenir of my visit I selected a well-preserved brick, which, by means of knotted handkerchiefs, I slung over my shoulder and so commenced the return journey. For three or four miles all went well, but after that the brick commenced to get rapidly heavier, until it became almost insupportable, while its constant tapping in the small of my back, caused by the jerky trot of the mule, was well-nigh intolerable. I tried to fasten it to the saddle, but, simple as it may seem, it would not hold, besides making the mule altogether unmanageable, so that after a desperate struggle for a few miles further I cast it from me with mingled feelings of disgust and thankfulness, and in all probability it remains in the same spot to this very day.

We reached Yang Fang before dark and much enjoyed a rest and some dinner, but as it was full moon and we were anxious to be back in Peking early next day, my friend proposed that we should press on for a couple of hours that evening.

With fresh ponies in place of the jaded mules, and feeling much happier on our doeskin saddles, we went along gaily for some distance, but the extreme cold and our own weariness soon began to tell, and we became so drowsy that we determined to off-saddle at the next inn. We had reckoned, however, without our host, for the inn was crammed full and we were obliged to take to the road once more, and that in no very amiable frame of mind. The next inn was if anything more crowded still, and the next, and the next. For five mortal hours we plodded on, more asleep than awake, and I retain but a misty recollection of the snow-covered ground, of my pony slipping while crossing a frozen ford, and of my continual efforts to keep in the saddle. At one in the morning we hammered at the doors of yet another inn, only to be again repelled with the frightful words, "All full."

My friend, who spoke the vernacular fluently, was now doing his best, and with such effect that the door was cautiously opened a few inches, when with one bound I was inside, and seeing a kang with only one man on it I tumbled him off and flung myself down, just conscious of acrid opium smoke, a great uproar and streams of the most insulting abuse.

On awaking I found my friend by my side still asleep and the morning well aired. The squalid inn was almost deserted, for the overnight lodgers had departed with their carts and pack-animals before dawn, so that I had not to face the individual whom I had so unceremoniously dispossessed of his bed, although I left a dollar for him with the innkeeper, knowing full well it would never reach him, but choosing thus to ease a somewhat guilty conscience.

We had not much further to go and were easily back in Peking before tiffin.

Another expedition I made that winter was to a burial-place of emperors of the late Ming dynasty, commonly known as the "Ming Tombs," consisting of several immense temples or pagodas possessing but little architectural beauty and now considerably dilapidated.

One of these temples is approached by an avenue of gigantic figures representing warriors, statesmen, horses, camels, elephants, etc., each figure apparently cut from a single block of stone.

As two hundred and sixty years ago the Chinese Mings were dispossessed by the present ruling Manchu dynasty, no attempt is now made to preserve these interesting monuments.

In summer the heat is often very great during the day, the thermometer frequently registering between ninety and a hundred degrees in the shade, and is rendered more trying by the unsanitary and neglected condition of the thoroughfares.

At night, however, it is so pleasantly cool that one can sleep under a blanket, while punkahs over the bed are never necessary as in the central provinces. Riding outside the city walls in the cool of early morning or late afternoon is then most enjoyable, many interesting sights affording constant diversion.

Acrobats practising their tours de force, tragedians with tense faces declaiming in a high falsetto to imaginary audiences, rag-pickers sorting their fulsome wares with iron-pointed sticks, herds of coarse, black swine being bought and sold, while in the shelter of the enormous buttresses archers erect paper targets some eight inches square and exercise their art with solemn dignity, elaborate posturing and considerable dexterity.

A good deal of tennis is played at the club and on the various private courts, though most of the diplomatic body as well as missionaries migrate during the great heat to temples in the Western Hills, which are about twelve miles from Peking, or, now that there is railway communication, to the seaside resort of Pei-Tai-Ho.

One afternoon another European and I rode some ten miles out of Peking to inspect the ruins of the celebrated Summer Palace, which, since its destruction in 1860 by the English and French forces, had remained a desolate and overgrown wilderness. Having put up the ponies at an inn, where an inquisitive old native wished to know whether our bright stirrups and bits were made of silver--the Chinese never dreaming of polishing their own--we proceeded on foot to the chief entrance, but as the work of restoration was then being commenced the gatekeeper refused us admission. Nothing daunted we strolled round to another side, and passing unobserved through a gap in the wall made careful inspection of a partially-destroyed pavilion overlooking a lake, interrupted only by a venerable guardian, who hobbled after us mildly requesting that we should depart. This we were preparing to do for another part of the extensive grounds, when suddenly we came into view of some scores of workmen who were engaged on the repairs. They stopped work and gazed at us but made no hostile move, and we could still have withdrawn in peace had not my companion, overcome by a desire to practise his Chinese, and in opposition to my urgent warning, advanced towards them with a beaming smile. No sooner was he within range than a shower of bricks and stones filled the air and we were both constrained to turn tail and make for the gap at full speed, closely followed by the howling mob. We did not pause before reaching the inn, and then only to secure our ponies and continue our undignified flight. I was uninjured, but my companion had received a nasty blow on the head, at which I secretly rejoiced, as owing to his action we had not only been exposed to considerable danger but had been prevented from further investigating a historical spot since strictly closed to all Europeans.

I left Peking at the close of 1889, and there being then no railway the ninety miles' journey to Tientsin had to be performed either on horseback, by cart along cross-country tracks or via the River Peiho, taking boat at Tungchow, which is fourteen miles from the capital. I decided on going by boat as being far more comfortable than the other alternatives.

Winter had begun early and there was already a certain amount of ice, but from inquiries made the river was still open. My baggage was piled on to a long, narrow cart drawn by two mules, while I and my boy each bestrode a very small donkey, and so I passed out from the mighty city by the stone road which leads to Tungchow, as owing to heavy rains and subsequent frost the more comfortable country tracks were impassable.

This road, or rather causeway, is another witness to the Chinese characteristic of constructing costly works and then leaving them thenceforth to fall into disrepair and ruin.

From twelve to fourteen feet in width, it is built of massive granite blocks a foot square by perhaps three to seven feet in length, and originally must have been a magnificent highway of perfect evenness. Time and the grinding wheels of heavy-laden carts, however, have worn innumerable ruts seven or eight inches deep into the solid stone, so that in passing over it a springless cart crashes from side to side with great violence, almost throwing shaft animals to the ground and rendering it quite impossible for any European to ride in the vehicle, while crockery or any other fragile article, however carefully packed, is doomed to certain destruction.

On arrival at Tungchow I saw a great deal of ice floating down with the current, but the boatmen declared, and I believe truly, that the river was still open to the sea, so having transferred the baggage to one boat, and embarking with my boy and pointer on another, we cast off at about three o'clock in the afternoon, expecting to reach Tientsin the following evening.

Before dark the ice greatly increased in quantity, and from the cabin where, enveloped in rugs, I was having tea, the boatmen's excited voices could be heard making frequent inquiries of upward-bound junks as to our prospects of getting through, for they were Tientsin men and anxious to get their boats home before the river was frozen up. At six o'clock, however, when we had covered about twelve miles and it was quite dark, the boats suddenly crashed into a barrier of ice, which had but just formed, effectually stopping our further progress. By frantic efforts and with great shoutings both craft were warped to within a few feet of the bank, and there we lay, each moment becoming more firmly wedged in by fresh ice hurrying down with the stream, and which, driven by pressure of the frozen impact, piled up against us with a horrid grinding noise until large sheets an eighth of an inch thick and as clear as crystal came gliding, as though alive, on to our decks.

There being no likelihood of our release I presently sent one of the crew back to Tungchow for carts with which to continue the journey, but to my dismay he returned at two in the morning with the intelligence that no carts could be hired.

The position was a disagreeable one, as it was imperative that I should reach Tientsin in time to catch a steamer for Shanghai before the close of navigation, so I started off the boy, accompanied by another boatman, with instructions to get a conveyance of some sort and at any cost. This attempt was more successful, for at ten o'clock they returned with a farmer and his truly wonderful cart, drawn by a pony, a cow and a donkey, but which they had only been able to hire for the exorbitant sum of forty dollars.

My goods and chattels were again transferred, and after making a present of five dollars to the disconsolate boatmen, we started off at something less than two miles an hour.

If I rode on the piled-up baggage I was quickly numbed by the cold. If I walked I soon left the cart far behind, yet dared not lose sight of it for fear of its taking another route, so that my time was spent in walking ahead and then retracing my steps to meet the cart.

Long after dark we halted at one of the usual wayside inns, a collection of hovels built round a dirty, open yard, filled with carts and animals, and the home of pigs and fowls, while I found accommodation on a brick bed in a comfortless room, or rather shed, with torn paper windows and uneven mud floor.

Swallowing some cold food by the light of a tallow candle guttering in the draught, I was too tired and too disgusted not to sleep, and by three o'clock next morning we were again crawling on our way beneath the blazing stars and chilled by a piercing wind.

All things have an end, and so after four days of absolute misery I arrived at noon, hungry, footsore and unwashed, at a friend's house in Tientsin and in time to catch the last steamer, which was sailing that night.

After a hot bath and a good tiffin I retired gratefully to bed, but, such is the callousness of human nature, only to be routed out at three o'clock to play in a football match, which, the Fates be praised, our side lost.

FOOTNOTES:

[1] Pe = North. Nan = South. King = Capital City.

CHAPTER VIII

HERE AND THERE

Of the three routes to China:

1. The overland, by rail through Europe and Siberia;

2. The westerly, across the Atlantic, North America and the Pacific;

3. The easterly, via the Mediterranean, Suez Canal, Red Sea and Indian Ocean,

the last is perhaps the most interesting and in many ways the most comfortable, for it is possible to take a magnificent mail steamer at an English port and remain on board, surrounded by as much comfort and luxury as is to be found in a first-class hotel, until you land in either Hongkong or Shanghai.

The finest of these vessels are veritable floating palaces, the saloons of which are gilded and decorated regardless of expense, richly carpeted, illuminated with electric light, cooled by electric fans, and where meals are served which would not demean any restaurant in London or Paris. Music-room, library, smoking-room and bar, laundry, barber's shop and delightful marble baths all find place.

On the crack German boats a band plays at frequent intervals, while I have actually seen cold stoves in some of the cabins, so that when passing through great heat in the Red Sea or elsewhere you could close your cabin door, draw up your chair and have a good cool.

I am not sure how these stoves are worked, but believe they are connected in some way with the refrigerator, which makes ice for use on board and provides cold storage for meat and fruits, and that a current of ether or cold air is pumped through them.

In appearance they resemble a French porcelain furnace, abutting on one side of the cabin, and by means of a regulator you are able to reduce the temperature almost to freezing point. Although undoubtedly very pleasant during intense heat, and invaluable for hospital purposes, I question if they will come into anything like general use, for it seems to me that instantaneous changes from a temperature of perhaps one hundred degrees on deck to say sixty degrees in the cabin cannot fail to produce bad effects on the health.

Travelling by the easterly route you meet the sun, which causes each day to be shortened. By the westerly route you go with the sun, which causes each day to be lengthened.

During the journey round the world the aggregate of these shortenings or lengthenings will amount to twenty-four hours, so that on arriving again in England by the easterly route you will have gained a day, and instead of its being Wednesday, as you might think, it would be Tuesday, wherefore you would be obliged to have two Wednesdays in one week. By the westerly route, on the contrary, you would lose a day, so that returning on a Wednesday by your reckoning you would find everyone else calling it Thursday, and the following morning you would be obliged to recognise as Friday.

To avoid such confusion the date is always regulated when crossing the Pacific.

Going east, the captain notifies that there will be two consecutive Mondays, or two Thursdays, as the case be, in order to use up the extra day.

Going west, on the other hand, one of the days in a week must be omitted, there being no time for it if you are to arrive in port on the proper date.

A common story told in this connection is that on a certain voyage from Vancouver to Hongkong some missionary passengers settled to hold service in the saloon at 10:30 a.m. on Sunday, and posted up a notice to that effect in the usual place at the head of the saloon stairs, but omitted to previously consult the captain or ask his permission.

The captain, having no desire to be ignored, even unintentionally, aboard his own ship, quietly regulated dates, the passengers next morning finding an official notice posted up immediately over that of the missionaries, saying that it would be Sunday until 10 a.m., after which it would be Monday, so that missionaries, Sunday and divine service were all simultaneously suppressed.

The most comfortable and the most restful travelling in the world that I know of is on board the large river steamers running up the Yangtse for six hundred miles from Shanghai to Hankow, and then transhipping to somewhat smaller vessels, for the additional four hundred miles to Ichang.

Scrupulously clean, good table, jovial captains, excellent Chinese stewards, electric light, luxurious saloons, state-rooms double the size of cabins on even the finest ocean liners, few passengers, no noise and no sea-sickness, you glide on day and night over calm waters in a dream-like peace, broken only for a short time every few hours by the necessary stopping at ports of call to work cargo, and at riverside stations for Chinese passengers, who, however, do not mingle with the Europeans, but have saloons set apart for their own exclusive use. Some of these boats were built in the golden days of the early sixties, upon American models, and were fitted up on a scale considerably reduced in newer vessels.

The large bathrooms on these older boats are a great feature of comfort, and so numerous as to be almost bewildering to strangers; in fact, I have heard that a nervous young man fresh from home was the victim of an untoward mishap by mistaking the captain's bathroom for the one belonging to his own cabin, when on dashing in, the door having evidently been insecurely fastened on the inside, he found himself face to face with the captain's wife in her bath. Retreat was naturally instantaneous, but the position was so serious that his only course was to at once seek the captain and explain. This awkward task he started to perform, though in considerable trepidation, and found the husband reading in his cabin, and who, after listening calmly to a recital of the details, laconically remarked, "Ah, she has a beautiful figure, has she not?"

And the incident was closed.

The compass has been known for many centuries to the Chinese, but in accordance with their strange habit of doing so many things in an exactly contrary manner to Europeans, they "box" it the reverse way to ourselves, speaking of an east-north or a west-south breeze, and so on.

The expressions "to the right" and "to the left" I have never heard, for it is the custom to say "go to the east-south" or to the "west-north," as the case may be. Even in cities, when asking your way, the natives will direct you by the points of the compass rather than by the names of the streets.

Chinese screws turn from right to left, which is the opposite way to our own, and of this I had a practical demonstration when, on returning one morning from the mountains, a chair-coolie surreptitiously abstracted my flask from the tiffin-basket and tried to unscrew the stopper to get at the whisky, but being ignorant of the different method, he in reality screwed it on tighter, till at last it broke off, and when some hours later, on board the steamer, I discovered my ruined flask, an array of teeth-marks deeply imbedded in the metal plainly told the guilty tale.

At Peking, when studying Chinese, my teacher would often come after dinner during the long winter evenings, when seated by a roaring fire we discussed for practice in talking any subjects of interest. Amongst many curious things which I thus heard the following has always puzzled me with the conjecture, "Can there possibly be any truth in it?"

I had that day purchased some fur rugs of no particular value, and not being sure whether they were of dog-skin or goat-skin, asked the teacher his opinion. What his reply was I do not remember, but the conversation having turned on the subject of furs in general, he told me that some rare wolf-skins were exceedingly costly from the fact that the wolves, after being caught by Mongol hunters, had been skinned alive and the skins dressed in a particular manner. Rugs made of these, he declared, on the approach to the house of wild animals, robbers or of any threatening danger, would bristle up as if still on the back of the live animal when angered, and so give timely warning to the inmates; for which reason they were so highly valued.

I have never seen what purposed to be such a skin, but repeat the story if only for its Oriental weirdness.

Water buffaloes are a striking feature in Chinese rural life, more especially in the central and southern provinces. With a carcase almost as large and devoid of hair as that of an elephant, they have very short legs, and are consequently but little taller than the ordinary ox. Carrying on their heavy skulls enormous, semi-circular horns, they have a ferocious aspect, but strangely enough are exceedingly timid and docile. In summer, for the sake of coolness and to avoid mosquitoes, they plunge into streams or mud-holes, and lie there for hours with only their muzzles and eyes above water. It is rather a pleasing sight to see one of these unwieldy, dangerous-looking brutes being led quietly along, by means of a thin string attached to its nose, by a wee native girl, who, when tired of walking, stops the animal, draws its head down by the string, places her tiny foot on the massive horn and is slowly raised from the ground by the buffalo and placed gently on his back, which is so broad that she can kneel and play about on it while her charge is grazing. These buffaloes are chiefly employed in the cultivation of rice, and as the flesh of oxen is but rarely eaten by the Chinese, they usually die of old age.

On one occasion I saw a large family of natives returning mournfully to their village from a neighbouring meadow, and on making inquiries was told that they had been to bury their water buffalo, which had just died after a faithful service of more than twenty years.

When on a shooting trip far up the River Han I saw a large buffalo with four boys on his back, grazing by the side of a water-ditch, which lay between him and a steep bank some ten feet high. The grass being very soft, my close approach was unobserved, until a hare getting up I fired off my gun. Instantly the buffalo dashed through the ditch and up the bank, when the boys, having nothing to hold on to except one another, were shot off backwards into the water, where they formed a perfect heap of struggling arms and legs, to my great amusement.

Chinese farm-houses are very different from the substantial, comfortable dwellings obtaining in this country, being primitive clay hovels with no upper storeys, having tile roofs, windows of oiled paper, and mud floors, while the furniture is home-made and of the roughest description. No walks or gardens surround the house, which stands in the centre of the farm-yard, outbuildings and cesspools, with the threshing-floor, as a rule, immediately outside the front door. Pigs, dogs, fowls and goats roam at will through the dwelling and about the premises, while the two or three buffaloes and oxen used for ploughing and threshing are tethered to neighbouring trees.

Although wheat, maize, barley and millet are largely cultivated in the north, rice is the principal crop wherever it can be grown, much water being necessary. It is first sown in quite a small, dry patch, to be subsequently transplanted, and comes up as thick as grass and of a most brilliant green. The fields, which rarely exceed half an acre, and are generally very much less, are now tilled. First, they are flooded by a careful system of irrigation to a depth of three or four inches, and when sufficiently soft turned over with a primitive, wooden plough, shod with a small iron blade or tip, and drawn by one water buffalo. After this they are harrowed, the farmer standing on the harrow and driving the buffalo as it wades along, until they are masses of rich, liquid mud. The young plants are now pricked out by hand, about six inches apart, and the fields kept just flooded by a constant stream of running water. When ripe the crop stands about two and a half feet in height, and the water having been cut off some time previously, reaping commences with the sickle.

Into the harvest-field is often brought a large wooden tub about four feet in diameter by three feet high, and the reaper, having cut an armful of rice, takes it by the straw end and threshes the ears five or six times with great force over the side, so that the grain falls into the tub, which, when thus filled, is replaced by an empty one and taken to the threshing-floor, where the contents are thrown up by shovels-full into the air, the breeze blowing the chaff to one side and the winnowed rice falling in a heap by itself. When the crop is not thus threshed in the harvest-field it is stacked at the farm, and sometimes in the low forks of large trees to remove it from the danger of possible floods, subsequently to be trodden out by oxen on the threshing-floor or beaten out by the farmer and his family with light basket-work flails on bamboo shafts.

In villages and small towns where many houses adjoin, it is a common practice to paint or dye young chickens as soon as they are hatched, so that each housewife may know her own. One woman will colour hers a bright red, another will use blue, another green, and so on, the appearance of these strikingly-coloured little creatures intermingled in the streets being exceedingly droll and novel to Europeans.

Amongst all classes of Chinese, from beggars to Academicians, belief in ghosts, dreams and the supernatural generally is absolute and unshakable.

If you express doubt or scepticism they will readily agree with you from a certain nervousness of being thought ridiculous, as well as from a feeling of the futility of any attempt to persuade Europeans of the soundness of such convictions.

In the autumn of 1899, when at Shasi, which is an unthriving town nine hundred miles up the Yangtse, and where another Englishman and I were the then only Europeans residing amongst a dense, hostile population, which only a few weeks previously had burnt down all foreign houses and forced the inmates to flee for their lives in small boats, two of the most remarkable cases of this universal superstition came directly under my notice.

At that time one of those rebellions which are a chronic feature of Chinese Society was in full bloom in the neighbouring province of Szechwan, where an individual named Y?Man-tze was heading a crusade against Christians and foreign influence, when at least one French father was slain and another held in prolonged captivity, despite all efforts of the local officials to effect his release.

The doings of this redoubtable brigand were naturally our chief topic of daily conversation, and a very intelligent and highly-educated Chinese gentleman, who kept me informed of local events, said that the natives generally credited him with mystic powers. "Of course," he added, eyeing me suspiciously, "it cannot be true, still, it is current gossip in all the tea-shops."

After a short pause I informed him confidentially that whatever other foreigners might or might not believe, I personally had considerable doubts as to the non-existence of supernatural agencies.

Without looking up I could feel that his eyes were critically scanning my face in search of ridicule or sarcasm, but I managed to preserve a stolid demeanour, and purposely dropping further discussion of the matter, went in search of cigars and stimulants to help us while away the afternoon. At length he again broached the subject, which I could see was of great interest to him, and warming to his theme under the influence of a sympathetic listener and good cheer, he finally told me in a burst of confidence and with low, excited voice, the following fact relative to Y?Man-tze.

At the outset of his lawless career this supernaturally gifted desperado, having collected a band of followers, fastened round their ankles such heavy weights that they were at first totally unable to move; but, as the fruit of continual exertions, they by-and-by managed to creep a few paces, later on they were able to walk easily, and finally even to run with their loaded feet.

The time for action having come, Y?Man-tze removed the weights, when his disciples were so buoyant that they could all fly, and so were able to pass rapidly between places far apart, and to successfully avoid all attempts at capture.

For those unacquainted with the East it is doubtless well-nigh impossible to credit that such rubbish as this could be implicitly believed by any considerable number of people, yet such was the case, and the fact that the Chinese government eventually bribed Y?Man-tze with official rank and a large sum of money to desist from his evil ways by no means tended to diminish the illusion.

For several weeks we were continually threatened with a visitation from some predatory band of Y?Man-tze's followers, so that when one stormy night two large fires simultaneously broke out in different parts of the town we thought trouble was at hand. Our anticipations, however, were happily unfulfilled, the storm having prevented the rebels from descending the river as intended, though the fires, which evidently had been previously planned and timed, were ignited.

Next morning my compatriot brought in word that he had visited the scenes of the conflagrations, and that three victims, who had been fearfully burnt, were lying in the street covered with straw mats, but still alive. Being without medical comforts of any description I was powerless to render assistance, so refrained from even quitting the house.

An hour later my countryman again rushed in, followed by two or three Chinese, to say that relatives of the sufferers had brought them to a piece of waste ground hard by, had heaped wood round them, had poured petroleum over them, and were now burning them as a sacrifice to the god of fire, he having already established his claim over them.

What could be done in the face of such horrifying circumstances? Nothing, for the poor wretches were already beyond any human aid, and to have interfered would have brought on us instant vengeance from the excited mob, but never, to the end of my days, shall I forget that sickening feeling of enforced inaction.

I especially record this incident as it is the only one of so extreme a nature that I have ever heard of as taking place amongst the Chinese, although it is a matter of common knowledge that they frequently refuse to rescue drowning persons for fear of displeasing the river god.

We subsequently learnt with much satisfaction that the rebels, to the number of two or three hundred, on being turned aside by the storm, crossed the border into the province of Hunan, and there, after murdering an official, his women-folk and some servants, were surrounded in a swamp on the shores of the Tongting lake by Government troops and butchered to a man.

Native breeds of swine are very coarse and always coal black, so that when a French friend of mine imported for the first time into Peking two white, foreign-bred pigs, they were objects of immense curiosity to the local Chinese, who thought them exceedingly uncanny, and considered it far from improbable that the departed spirits of former friends might well have migrated into forms so passing fair.

After they had been carefully fattened, a kiddier was sent for to give them the happy dispatch, but no sooner had he set eyes on his quarry than he scuttled off in alarm, and nothing would induce him to return, nor could any other butcher be prevailed upon to officiate, so that, my friend declared, he was obliged to roll up his sleeves and perform the gruesome, though necessary operation himself.

"Old custom" is almost a religion with the celestials, to subvert which requires great caution, persistency and strength. If anything can be justified by old custom, or even precedent, it is considered to be unassailable, no matter how harmful or irrational it may be.

Take the matter of foot-binding.

Laws have been passed, and are still extant, expressly forbidding this cruel and senseless habit, and the ruling race, the Manchus, have never practised it, still the Chinese, and the women more than the men, cling to it with fanatical stubbornness for the sole reason that it is old custom, and that if girls' feet were not bandaged it would outrage the universal sense of propriety.

I have frequently talked the subject over with Chinamen, who readily acknowledge that it is useless, besides being extremely painful to young children, but they say if their daughters had natural feet they would most probably fail to get husbands, as no man wishes his wife to be in any way extraordinary or different from other women. "In any case," they frequently retort, "we do not know that foot-binding gives much more pain than do the tight-laced stays of foreign women, and certainly it is not so ugly or prejudicial to the health."

The Chinese, contrary to ourselves, look back to the past for inspiration and guidance, and to concern oneself about novelty or change appears to them as savouring strongly of shiftiness and want of tone.

A curious instance of how quickly precedent can be established, and of its binding force, came to my notice some years ago at Peking.

At a certain point the now shallow waters of the moat encircling the city wall had for long years been spanned by a foot-bridge, but which, having become rotten and weak, duly crumbled away.

With Oriental dilatoriness no attempt was made to rebuild it for some months, and it was then found that two men, who during the interval had been earning a livelihood by wading to and fro carrying pedestrians between the opposite banks, strongly objected to a new bridge on the ground that it would take away their occupation now fairly established. Backed by numerous relatives and by public opinion, these two miserable coolies had successfully resisted the proposed reconstruction when I left the capital, and it is highly probable that they or their sons still monopolise passenger traffic at the ford.

To many even in this country, and to far more on the Continent, where Christmas is observed solely as a religious festival, the New Year with its train of bills, gifts, junketings and holidays is a period of abomination, when all business is dislocated and servants run mad.

At such places in the East as Hankow, where a considerable Russian colony exists, there are three New Years of progressive virulence. The first of January is observed by all Europeans as a general holiday, when the ladies stay at home to preside over elaborate teas, at which all gentlemen of their acquaintance are expected to appear if only for a few minutes, while the men, both married and single, taking a large supply of cards, sally forth to call at the house of each lady in turn to wish her a Happy New Year, a proceeding which takes up several hours and necessitates a surprising amount of endurance. Dinners, dances, complimentary visits from Chinese friends, and other social functions help to swell the list of New Year obligations.

Things have scarcely settled down again when the Russian New Year is at hand, for in the dominions of the White Czar time is still reckoned by the old style, and as Russians are particularly keen and very pronounced in their observance of anniversaries and fêtes, the place is again turned topsy-turvy for several days beneath floods of excellent sweet champagne.

The Chinese calendar marches coeval with the moons, which fact generally places their New Year some time in February, the exact date fluctuating from year to year to the extent of three or four weeks.

The last few days of the old year is a great time of reckoning, when all outstanding debts must be paid so as to commence the New Year with a clean slate, and woe to the man who fails to meet his obligations.

From faces clouded with anxiety during this trying period there is a sudden revulsion on the stroke of midnight to countenances wreathed in smiles, as for weal or woe the New Year is ushered in with deafening fusillades of fire-crackers and a great beating of gongs. In the morning all China is astir betimes, dressed in gala attire and interchanging congratulatory visits. Business is entirely suspended for several days, it being the one great annual holiday, and it is extremely difficult to get even your own servants to pay so much as a minimum of attention to their household duties; in fact, I yearly register a mental vow not to lose my temper with them on any account during New Year week, for besides being useless it would probably entail the additional discomfort of having to engage and train new hands.

At this season native officials as well as merchants are in the habit of making presents indicative of good-will to those foreigners with whom they have business relations.

Your boy brings in a bright red visiting-card eight inches by three, coming from an official who begs you will deign to accept his best wishes for the New Year, together with a few trifling presents. Immediately three or four coolies arrive, groaning as loudly as possible beneath the weight of hams, boxes of cigars, jars of dried fruits, boxes of tea, oranges and champagne. You inspect the presents with exclamations of appreciation and then privately consult the boy as to what you should retain, it being the general practice to return the greater part. A box of tea, a jar or two of dried fruits, some oranges and perhaps a box of cigars are selected, while a few dollars are presented to the coolies, by whom you forward in return your own Chinese card to the official with seasonable wishes and thanks for his thoughtful kindness.

As I was reading by my fire one afternoon in Shanghai the door was quietly opened, two hands gently pushed an enormous live turkey into the room and the door was again closed. The turkey commenced to stalk about with an occasional gobble. After watching the intruder for a few seconds I started to catch him, but found it was no easy matter. He flew on to the sideboard, from there to the mantelpiece and then to the window-sill, scattering knick-knacks and photographs far and wide. He ran under the sofa and table, finally escaping into my bedroom, where, with a desperate effort, I caught him by his legs under the bed. While dragging him out he beat his wings with great force, and as the bed had evidently not been swept under for months, drove forth such a cloud of dust and fluff as to almost choke me, while filling the whole room.

Round his neck was tied a red label bearing New Year greetings from a Chinese merchant.

The entire boating population cease work at New Year, and tying up their craft in convenient places give themselves up to such few pleasures as their primitive mode of life allows.

At Macao, hundreds of fishing-boats, which supply the market both there and at Hongkong, assemble and anchor close together in orderly rows, both in the inner harbour as well as in the bay facing the Praia Grande, under strict supervision of the Portuguese authorities. Mat awnings are erected over the decks, thus forming commodious rooms, which are decorated with scrolls and lanterns, and in which feastings and family gatherings take place for several days, after which the whole fleet, gaily decked with flags, puts again to sea.

Fish of any kind is a favourite article of food, and the methods of catching them are extremely numerous. Otters, cormorants, nets, baskets and hooks without bait, all meet with due measure of success, but by far the most remarkable manner of fishing was that which I saw from the bows of a steamer made fast to the hulk at Hankow.

It was mid-winter and bitterly cold, the ground being covered with almost a foot of snow. I had been to tiffin with the captain and was just coming away when, pointing to some natives in a sampan close alongside, he said, "Have you ever seen those men dive for fish?"

I never had, and being glad of the opportunity, stopped to watch. There were three men in the boat, of whom one worked the paddles, while the other two, stark naked, crouched on the forepart, sheltering themselves from the biting wind with an old straw mat. Having come to a suitable spot, where the depth may have been from ten to fifteen feet, the boat was stopped, and the two divers instantly plunged into the turbid water, to reappear some seconds later with a live fish in each hand, while one of them had also a third fish in his mouth. The diving was repeated several times with varying results before I took my leave, and the captain assured me that this was a common sight on the Yangtse in winter, when the fish were probably lying in the mud torpid from the cold.

When returning to Kiukiang from a fortnight's shooting trip in the neighbourhood of Ngankin, my boat was much delayed by light and contrary winds, which frequently obliged us to anchor in order to avoid being swept back by the strong current. On one of these occasions three of the crew took the jolly-boat and rowed ashore, a distance of some hundred yards, and while smoking on deck I could see them wading along by the bank, groping in the mud and occasionally putting something into a bucket which they had taken with them. Questioned as to what they were doing, the lowdah replied, "Fishing," and my astonishment was not diminished when they returned on board with the bucket half-filled with fine perch, varying from perhaps eight ounces to a pound in weight. Until then I was unaware that perch existed in Chinese waters, nor have I since seen any.

The nearest approach to this kind of fishing that I know of is down in my old home amongst the Norfolk broads, where on warm days, when lying in the weeds, tench can be tickled with the fingers and caught by a sudden nip behind the gills; but the art requires intimate knowledge of local waters, much patience and great skill.

One of the most frequent questions that I am asked at home is, "Do not Chinamen wear the finger-nails very long?" They do. Scholars perform no manual labour, in visible token of which they allow the nails of the left hand to grow an inch or an inch and a half in length, but the nails on the right hand, while also long, are short in comparison with those on the left.

To be classed with literary or educated men is the greatest of all considerations, for which reason there is always a tendency for anyone and everyone to wear a long coat and to don huge tortoise-shell-rimmed spectacles, such as are affected by the literati, as well as to cultivate the nails of the left hand. As the use of the word esquire has degenerated in this country until not to apply it to all and sundry is considered to be almost a snub, so the habit of wearing long finger-nails in China has descended through every rank of Society until it is now more often the badge of envious imitation than of any scholarly attainments. So precious to the owners are these claw-like nails that I have often seen them protected by silver sheaths, and have heard that for cases of extraordinary growth the whole of the left hand is even carried in a bag.

There is much outcry in these latter days against the newly-formed habit of cigarette smoking cultivated by ladies of the West. Condemnation of the practice seems if anything to act as an incentive, so, yielding to the pleasant temptation of palliating faults in pretty women, I would suggest as an excuse that they are but following in the foot-steps of their sisters of the Far East, where, it may be roughly stated, the women-folk of a third of the human race smoke pipes.

I cannot say that very young girls appear to indulge much, though women of all ages do to a great extent, inhaling the smoke and puffing it through the nose in thick clouds. The pipes in general use are either small brass ones, having straight wooden stems a foot in length, with clumsy porcelain mouthpieces, or brass water-pipes, which when being smoked make an unpleasant gurgling sound. The bowl of either kind is so tiny that it will only hold a pinch or two of very fine tobacco, which three or four whiffs consume, when it has to be refilled and lighted from a slow-match held ready in the hand until the smokeress has smoked enough. The picture is neither winsome nor sweet.

The Chinese have very few amusements corresponding to our outdoor games, although at treaty-ports, and in those places where there are any roads, men are taking readily to cycling, albeit, from the flowing nature of their garments they generally use ladies' bicycles. Of these few pastimes archery is considered the most distingu? while boys attain to great skill in playing shuttlecock with their feet, being able to keep up the feathered cork for a dozen or twenty times, and passing it considerable distances from one to another. Judge then of my surprise when, on asking a young Chinaman at Peking how he had spent his holiday of the previous day, he replied quite naturally that he had passed the afternoon at his cricket club.

I could hardly believe my ears, for as far as I knew a game of cricket had never been played at Peking, even by Englishmen, there being no suitable ground, and it was only by plying him with questions that I elicited it was the cricket of the hearth to which he alluded, and that his club was a gambling-house to which young men brought their crickets, there to fight grim duels in a basin for the championship, while noble owners staked considerable sums on the prowess of their diminutive gladiators and stimulated their energies by tickling them with straws.

On all the waterways of China enormous flocks of tame ducks are to be seen. These flocks generally number several thousands of birds each and are carefully herded by the duck farmer and his sons, who swim them about from place to place in search of suitable feeding-grounds. On the Yangtse I have seen them in mid-stream floating down in compact masses with the racing current and surrounded by their guardians in tubs, who, armed with long bamboos, smartly whack any bird which may happen to stray away from the flock until it rejoins its companions.

These ducks are apparently always of one age, be it a month, three months or full-grown, which fact had ever been a source of mild surprise to me, in view of the number of simultaneous broods which would be necessary to hatch off such swarms, until the matter was explained.

A friend of mine gave a tiffin party of four good men and true on his stern-wheel house-boat, the motive power for which was supplied by half-a-dozen coolies driving the wheel with their feet, on the same principle as the tread-mill, and we were gliding up the Taipa Channel near Macao at about four knots, when suddenly our craft came into a sea of egg-shells sailing gaily before the breeze and having at a short distance much the appearance of water-lilies.

For a quarter of an hour or so we ploughed through these shells, which must have numbered tens of thousands, making various conjectures as to their origin, until our host, who had been below superintending the icing of the champagne, came on deck and explained that they undoubtedly were from an incubator in which ducks had just been hatched. This was new to me, so I asked him for details, but he replied that beyond knowing of the incubators and that they were made of manure and lime in which eggs were buried until hatched, he had not been able to procure further information.

Since then I have made many inquiries, but the Chinese will reveal little beyond the fact that incubators "have always existed" for the hatching of ducks and geese.

A gentleman whose knowledge of the Chinese and their ways is unsurpassed has also kindly tried to find out, but with limited success, for, he says, it is regarded as a trade secret and the duck farmers will not divulge the process. However, he ascertained that the hatching takes place in early spring, when "a kind of primitive incubator is used. The eggs are placed in a big basket covered with straw or cotton wool, about a thousand eggs in one basket. Under this basket a charcoal fire is lit to keep the required temperature. The work is carried on in closed rooms and one man is always in attendance turning the eggs. Only eggs of ducks and geese are thus treated."

Whether these incubators are made of manure and lime in the open air, whether they are in rooms heated by charcoal fires, or whether there are both kinds, the interesting fact is established that incubators "have always existed" in China, while results, as seen in the huge flocks of ducks, proclaim them as thoroughly successful. And this, too, when it has been unreservedly believed that the incubator was a modern triumph of Western science!

Another little matter has attracted my attention. There have lately been paragraphs in several papers announcing the excellent results obtained from a new system of registering criminals by means of thumb-marks.

Thumb-marking may be new to Scotland Yard, but in China it is a very ancient practice. I have seen illiterate men smear their thumbs with ink and make impressions at the foot of documents, such thumb-marks being accepted as in every way equivalent to full signatures.

CHAPTER IX

THE MARRIAGE TIE

In the province of Kiangsi on the banks of the River Kan, which flows almost due north to the Poyang lake and so into the Yangtsekiang, is situate the town of Kanchow, on the outskirts of which dwelt a merchant named Chin Pao-ting with his wife and infant son.

After the custom of all Chinese merchants, Mr Chin had a shop which, although used for retail purposes, was in reality the office of his not inconsiderable wholesale business. Mr Chin had some time previous to this date, the early spring of 1892, engaged a young man of the locality named Wang Foo-lin, as accountant and confidential clerk, and he had proved himself so intelligent and useful that not only did Chin regard him with feelings of friendship but even conceived the idea of subsequently taking him into partnership. What Chin's particular business was I do not know, beyond the fact that each year it took him away from home for several weeks, and sometimes months at a time, when he travelled to other provinces. This annual voyage was now at hand. Four boats were filled with various kinds of merchandise, while a fifth and smaller craft was selected to convey Chin and his assistant, who now accompanied his master for the first time. This boat was fairly comfortable from a Chinese point of view, having benches on either side of the cabin and a kind of platform at the back, with a small, low table thereon bearing the customary incense-burner, containing fragrant joss-sticks, and also on this occasion a small joss or gilt image of Buddha, which Chin always took with him on his wanderings.

All preparations having been slowly completed the day for departure arrived, and Chin, with much bowing and ceremonial posturing, having wished his wife and little son adieu, embarked with Wang, taking the equivalent of five thousand dollars[2] in sycee shoes and gold-dust, and amidst valedictory fusillades of fire-crackers, as well as a beating of gongs, the flotilla cast off and sailed away down river.

Nothing of particular interest occurred during the voyage of two hundred miles to the Poyang lake beyond usual delays caused by the dried-up condition at that season of all waterways connected with China's mighty river.

The sources of the Yangtse are to be found in the mountain ranges of Thibet, and as during winter and early spring the deep snows of those lofty regions lie icebound and the great river is fed only by local rains, its waters dwindle in volume until they find a level forty feet below that of summer and autumn, when torrid heat and torrential rains thaw the snows in Central Asia and fill the river-bed with a thick, brown current which, after overflowing into and filling all lakes, tributaries and unprotected lowlands in the Yangtse valley, sweeps eastwards to the ocean, a foaming torrent of irresistible force.

After about twenty days of incessant toil in tracking, poling and yulowing along the tortuous and mud-bound channel of the Kan, where sailing, owing to the low water and consequent towering banks which shut off the wind, was seldom possible, the small fleet emerged on the Poyang lake. Not, however, the magnificent sheet of water which is found there in summer, but the lake as it is in winter, contracted to one tenth of its maximum size, and little more than a wide and sluggish river flanked by boundless mud tracts swarming with snipe and wildfowl. Another few days' sailing, for the breeze could now be felt across the wide marshland, and Hukow (mouth of the lake) was reached, where the merchandise in the four small lake boats was transferred to a large and stately junk destined to carry it far up-river towards the West, while good accommodation was found on board both for Chin and his assistant. As soon as the transhipment of cargo had been completed, and Chin had written a letter for transmission to his wife by the boats returning to Kanchow, sail was made on the junk, and passing out of the tranquil waters of the lake she was seen to shape an up-river course reefed close before a rising gale, until lost to sight in the rain and gathering darkness.

The empty boats arrived in due course at Kanchow, when the letter was faithfully delivered, and this being the last communication that would be received from her husband prior to his return, Mrs Chin resigned herself to many weeks of dreary loneliness.

Weeks lengthened into months, and the waiting woman began to feel anxious as to the well-being of her lord.

The stifling, burning summer came and went, and still there was neither sign nor tidings of the absent one.

Inquiries made of passing junks, to the crews of many of which Chin was well-known, ever elicited the invariable reply that nothing had been seen or heard of him.

Autumn and winter still brought no tidings, and the poor, saddened woman yielded to the conviction that some disaster had overtaken her husband and that she would see him no more.

Early Chinese marriages are almost invariably arranged by the parents, the young folks, even if old enough, having no voice in the matter. Later on, plurality of wives, though far from universal, is also quite common and of good repute.

The lower orders generally have only one wife, not being able to afford more, although as soon as a man commences to prosper and rise in the social scale his first thought is to procure by contract or by purchase an additional helpmeet, who, however, ranks far below the first or No. 1 wife. Similarly No. 2 ranks before No. 3, and so on. Four or five wives is a common number in well-to-do households, though one old friend of mine, since dead, had taken to himself sixteen.

Husbands regard the marriage tie as binding on them chiefly with regard to the material well-being of the family, whereas the honour of the family rests on the wife's steadfastness in maintaining sacred the nuptial vow, any detected laxity in this respect being visited on her with remorseless punishment both by her libidinous husband and by the whole of his clan. Widows seldom marry again, it being the duty and pride of a virtuous woman to remain faithful to the memory of her dead husband. Throughout the whole length and breadth of China memorial arches to widows who have been faithful to their troth till death are to be seen in almost every village.

Mrs Chin may have been, and probably was, attached to her husband with that fanatical single-mindedness which belongs to women of the East. She may have considered it her bounden duty only. Whether love or duty furnished the motive I cannot tell, but after making all possible inquiries to no purpose she determined to set out herself and search for traces of the missing one. The shop and her belongings were sold to provide money for the way, and the poor woman, forsaking all and carrying the child strapped to her shoulders, turned with a bitter heart from her former prosperous home to face the world on her well-nigh hopeless quest. Of her wanderings I could get no record, and she would probably, with Oriental inscrutability, have refused to even talk about them, but wherever else they may have led her, in the bitter winter of 1893 she was twenty miles up-river from Hukow at the open port of Kiukiang and alone, her child having perished by the way, begging food and prosecuting her inquiries. Chance led her to shelter for a night in the ruined but beautiful pagoda which stands high above the river on the cliff outside the city wall. To the old Buddhist hermit in possession she told her oft-repeated tale, only once again to receive the usual negative reply.

In the morning, however, as she was moving off on her daily trudge, the hermit appeared, and after the customary Buddhistic salutation, "O me tor foo,"[3] had been exchanged, he remarked that during the night it recurred to him that about eighteen moons had passed since he found the dead body of a man cast up naked on the opposite beach, and that following the rule of his order for acquiring merit he had carefully and reverently buried it.

The poor wanderer seemed at last to see some faint possibility of reward for her dreary pilgrimage. She followed the hermit to the river side, where his small and leaky sampan was drawn up on the mud. After considerable effort the boat was launched by the feeble pair, and taking her place in it she was rowed by the old man across the heaving river, which is here more than a mile in width, to the opposite beach, where a little above high-water mark the grave was found. Scraping aside the loose sand and rubble, and raising the unfastened lid of the rough coffin, the mouldering skeleton was unrecognisable. Quick as thought the woman thrust her fingers into the crumbling mass and raised an arm of the dead, on which was seen to be the half of a jade bracelet. Immediately baring her own arm to the hermit's gaze she displayed on it the other half of the same jewel.

A common Chinese practice is for man and wife to have one jade bangle split so as to form two bangles, and to wear one each, with much the same idea as our Mizpah rings.

The woman looked as if turned to stone. She moved not a muscle, but with livid face and hard, glassy eyes kept her position in the open grave, leaning on one hand across the coffin and grasping with her other the mouldering arm of the corpse, so that the two bangles were laid side by side.

Silently and reverently the old hermit stole away, leaving the living with the dead, and rowed back across the river to his home without once turning his eyes, for curiosity he had none, but in its place the Oriental's deep and mystic knowledge of life and death.

In the lonely grave amongst the rank grass and sand mounds the woman stayed, oblivious of the cold and soaking rain. For a long time she rested absolutely motionless as if also dead. Then a few upward movements of the head told of her silent agony. By-and-by a low, tremulous moan broke from her ashen lips. Almost inaudible at first, her sobs increased until her whole frame was convulsed. She called upon her husband, she poured blessings on his name, she craved blessings from his spirit. Long and loud, with all her soul, with all her strength and in most absolute sincerity, she bewailed her dead, as is the custom in the East, until exhaustion overpowered her and she slept.

It was almost dark when the hermit returned and thus found the faithful woman, sodden by the rain, her hair unbound and trailing in the sand. Gently rousing her and speaking soothing words he held out his humble offering of two little bowls containing rice and samshu, some sticks of incense and a few tiny candles. These the poor woman took, but without a sign, for her gratitude was too deep to show, and reverently placed the bowls, the lighted candles and smouldering incense-sticks in position round the grave.

Then, having kowtowed many times before the corpse, the lid of the coffin was replaced and covered with a few inches of sand, after which she turned as one in a trance and followed the hermit to his boat. Her husband was dead, she had bewailed him and burnt incense at his grave, and what further could this poor, broken woman do?

What her intentions then were I do not know, but a few days later, when returning at dusk from Kiukiang to the pagoda, she was stopped in a lonely alley outside the western gate by a man who said, "Your husband was murdered eighteen moons ago by Wang Foo-lin, who is now living in Hankow." It was too dark to see the man's face and the voice she did not know, but it was probably one of the sailors of the missing junk who had some grievance to avenge. From the effect these words had on the woman's fallen strength it might have been a message from the gods pointing afresh the path of duty. She sought her friend the hermit and related to him what had befallen her, and explained that she would now go to Hankow in quest of the murderer, for that her husband's spirit could never rest until his assassin had been brought to justice.

How she travelled the one hundred and twenty miles from Kiukiang to Hankow I do not know, but it is certain that she appeared in the latter place begging from house to house, and after a time recognised Wang Foo-lin trading under an assumed name in a shop of considerable size. Wang on his part did not recognise the feeble and unkempt old beggar-woman, so changed was she from the prosperous Mrs Chin, and took but little notice of this one amongst many tens of other mendicants, so that she was able to stand for some time at the shop door without attracting undue attention, when she carefully noted the contents of the store, and amongst other things recognised the gilt joss which her husband had taken with him. Her next step was to procure an audience of the local magistrate, and to do this she was obliged to expend a considerable part of her remaining cash in bribing the yam 衙 underlings ere they would consent to lay her case before the official or give her admittance to his court. After waiting many days the audience was granted, and kneeling on the filthy floor before the judgment seat she unfolded her story, accusing Wang Foo-lin of the murder of her husband. The magistrate listened to her tale, but at the end said, "You accuse this man of murder but produce no evidence in support of your statements, and your bare word is not sufficient. If you can bring forward any actual proof I will then take action." Mrs Chin replied that in Wang's shop she had seen a gilt image of Buddha which her husband had taken with him on his ill-fated voyage. That many years ago at Kanchow she had knocked over and broken the nose off this same image, and that to repair the damage she had melted down one of her gold earrings and replaced the nose. If, therefore, it were found that this gilt joss had a gold nose then the magistrate would know her tale was true. The official replied that he would accept this as sufficient evidence and would at once put it to the test. Sending his runners with Mrs Chin to the shop, Wang was arrested, and together with the gilt joss taken to the yam 阯, where it was quickly found that the image actually had a gold nose as declared by the old woman.

Knowing his case to be hopeless, and yielding to the racking torture which was quickly applied, the guilty wretch made a full confession of his crime. As a boy he had often heard of Chin Pao-ting's annual voyages to the West, while local gossip had so enlarged upon the merchant's wealth that the junk bearing him and his merchandise might well be a veritable treasure ship, so that when still a youth Wang had journeyed to Kiukiang with the deliberate intention of forming a scheme to waylay the annual expedition and thus acquire riches at a single stroke. As attendant in an opium den near the quay, he had come in contact with many low and desperate characters, amongst whom was the lowdah of a certain junk which plied for hire between the Poyang lake and the provinces of the West.

Gradually an intimacy sprang up between these two, until at length the diabolical plot was hatched of murdering Chin and levanting with his goods. Wang now returned to Kanchow, and, as we have seen, not only contrived to enter the service of Chin Pao-ting but also to gain his esteem and confidence.

For the next annual voyage a large river-junk to await the merchant at Hukow was, through Wang's astuteness, chartered on exceptionally favourable terms.

This junk, needless to say, was that of Wang's confederate, and once on board the unhappy traveller was a doomed man. On the first night of the voyage he was pounced on in his sleep, stunned with a blow and thrown overboard. At Kiukiang, where the vessel stopped, the lowdah and his men went ashore after receiving the gold dust and sycee shoes as their share of the plunder, while Wang, taking the junk and cargo as his portion, shipped a fresh crew and sailed on to Hankow, where he set up in business with the proceeds of his ill-gotten gains.

His examination finished and released from torture, Wang was led away in a swooning condition to a foul dungeon, where his silk garments were quickly stripped off and replaced by crimson clothes, stiff with clotted human blood and thick with vermin, but such as criminals condemned to execution are compelled to wear. By an iron ring mercilessly forced through his flesh and welded round his collar-bone he was chained to a stone pillar, and so left to await his doom or to rot on the reeking floor.

After prolonged deliberations amongst the authorities, it was decided that the prisoner should be beheaded at Kiukiang, that being the centre of the district in which his crime was committed.

Still clad in crimson clothes, the poor wretch was dragged by the chain from his cell, too emaciated and broken to even stand. His hands and feet were bound together with sharp cords and a bamboo pole thrust between them, and in such manner he was carried through the streets by two coolies, escorted by a few runners, to be thrown like a bundle of old clothes into the hold of a police junk, which bore him more dead than alive on his last voyage.

Owing to information extracted from Wang two further arrests were made of members of the junk's crew, but the lowdah and one other succeeded in making good their escape.

* * * * *

It was now summer, and the view looking south from Kiukiang city wall was peaceful and grand. In the distance rose the majestic Lushan range, the peaks of which were illumined by the setting sun. Nearer, the low hills, clothed with firs and azaleas, rolled as a carpet to the lake, which lay between them and the city ramparts. A narrow causeway from the city to the hills, cut the lake in two. At the far end of the causeway was a plot of level ground, strewn with potsherds and heaps of refuse. Here, in contrast to its usual solitude, a dense crowd had collected in evident anticipation of some interesting event. Presently two or three horsemen and a motley gang of soldiers emerged from the city and proceeded quickly along the causeway. Closely following were coolies carrying three red burdens, on bamboo poles, and these in turn were followed by more soldiers and a few officials in sedan chairs. It was an execution. The hurrying cavalcade was swallowed up in the dense crowd which happily served as a curtain to hide this ghastly scene of human wrath from Nature's smiling landscape. Half-an-hour later the official procession returned as quickly as it went, and gradually the crowd, sauntering by the water's edge, laughing, joking and making merry of the gruesome spectacle just witnessed, filtered back through the city gates.

Next morning three wooden baskets on long poles were exposed from the top of an archway, and in each basket was a human head. Wang and his companions had met their just rewards.

At Kanchow a pylow, or memorial arch, will eventually be erected in honour of the widow of Chin Pao-ting, so that to posterity may be preserved a just record of her virtuous devotion.

FOOTNOTES:

[2] Then about ?00.

[3] Untranslatable. "Peace be with you," or meaning to that effect.

CHAPTER X

DISCUSSED POINTS

"How do you like the Chinese?" is the most common of all queries, yet each time it is made I have to reflect as to what my answer shall be.

While unable to say that I like them, for, speaking collectively, they are an untaking, unlikeable people, still they possess many qualities and traits of character which per se must recommend them to all unprejudiced observers.

The chief hindrance to a better understanding with them is their rooted antipathy to ourselves, generated by our pushing, masterful ways. With but few and unimportant exceptions they do not want us, and would be glad to see the last of all Europeans, together with their civilisation, their missionaries and their trade. This is not very flattering, accustomed as we are to regard ourselves somewhat in the light of pearls before swine, but it is the truth. On the other hand, we know that our footing in the country was gained and is maintained by force, which knowledge, in addition to that pressure of silent enmity of which we are at all times conscious, brings our minds into a hostile attitude vis-?vis the Chinese. We are always in a state of antagonism, be it defensive or offensive. This mutual dislike, helped by the utterly different modes of life existing amongst Europeans and Asiatics, renders all other than business intercourse not only irksome but well-nigh impossible. Their ways not being our ways we do not want to know them intimately, and they on their part do not want to know us, wherefore, by tacit consent, we keep rigidly apart in social matters.

Many people seem to imagine the Chinese as being romantic, artistic, quaint, effeminate and uncanny.

Romantic they most certainly are not, but look at things with a brutal realism, of which their pet quotation is truly emblematical: "A man's greatest pleasure is found in reading his own essays and in making love to his neighbours' wives."

Of their artistic qualities there are many favourable critics, though personally I consider them to be extremely poor. Their music, both vocal and instrumental, is worse than rubbish; in sketching and painting they are without sense of perspective; their architecture is clumsy and coarse; their much-vaunted pottery is full of flaws and blemishes, for which reason a perfect specimen is almost priceless and over which connoisseurs hypnotise themselves; dancing, except by flower-girls, is unknown; while in literature they are safe from adequate criticism, owing to the impossibilities of their language. Embroidery, bronzes, carving, and dyeing in both pottery and silks are, in my opinion, their best artistic productions, although it is said that the famous colouring of chinaware is now a lost art, as those clans which held the secrets were almost extirpated during the Taiping rebellion. Many articles of vertu are undoubtedly valuable, but is it not rather owing to their antiquity, to their rarity, or to the fact that they are good specimens of a certain workmanship, however bad, rather than to any inherent artistic merits?

Quaint they indeed are from a European standpoint, but on more intimate knowledge this quaintness resolves itself into a slavish adaptability to the smallest circumstances in their daily struggle for existence. To a man who has been some years in the country, and who has tried to understand local conditions, the Chinese live on a dead level with matters of fact.

To say that they are effeminate would be incorrect. In some things, from our point of view, they undoubtedly are; in others they are extremely virile.

The captain of a British man-of-war told me that he considered them to be the poorest fighters in existence. That they habitually make a feeble show in battle cannot be gainsaid, but then they are a most matter-of-fact people, without any craving for military glory, and knowing beforehand that there is no possible chance of success, take time by the forelock and run away to escape a useless death.

Select one of our very best regiments and stop their pay for several months, deprive them of officers, take away all doctors and medical comforts, half starve them, arm them with flags, pikes and muzzle-loaders, and then march them against a crack European regiment. You may be sure the Chinese example would be quickly followed. I do not say the Chinese are brave, but I do believe that, given a good training, just treatment and a fair chance of success, they would prove no mean antagonists.

Possessing great natural aptitude, if it is made worth their while they will quickly become good riders, good shots, good at billiards and tennis, good sailors, etc., giving their whole attention to each matter, though without enthusiasm. It is this dull concentration on particular callings which has deprived their character of that vital force, initiative, which, while the greatest of safeguards to rival nations, has removed from the Chinese mind the power to comprehend and carry out large and complicated undertakings involving the handling and direction of modern systems and appliances. The Chinaman is at present content to supply labour, but whether in time he will be capable of also supplying the versatile, directing brain is a moot question. Anyhow, it will not be for long years and until he has lived under a modernised Government for several generations.

Extreme consideration for infancy and old age, the growing of long finger-nails, the supposed debilitation arising from opium-smoking, the universal usage of fans, the wearing of flowing garments and braided hair, and the discharging of domestic duties which in other countries fall to the lot of women, are probably largely accountable for the charges of effeminacy.

As to their uncanniness there is no doubt. We do not, and never shall, fathom the depth of a Chinaman's brain. After mutually looking at the same object from widely-different points of view we express our ideas, talk them over and invite criticism, while he--is silent. He listens to us and agrees, but keeps his own views to himself. We want to explain everything; he does not, but takes things on faith.

In our inmost hearts we generally do not feel sure whether we believe or do not believe in spiritualism, in good spirits, bad spirits, ghosts, dreams, devils and manifestations. He believes in them all without a suspicion of doubt, but, knowing our wonted thoughtless scepticism, will frequently say he does not, as the easiest way of avoiding a useless discussion and condemnation of established facts.

In dealing with educated Chinese many foreigners assume a forced, artificial manner, as though addressing themselves to an autocrat or a murderer, and are ever on the lookout for something to find fault with. My own idea is to maintain a naturally polite bearing and treat them precisely as you would your own countrymen of whatever rank in life. They strike me as being extremely responsive, and oftentimes even grateful for being taken simply as men and not as extraordinary specimens of another humanity.

The dominating factor of their lives is "face." Whatever happens, so long as a man can save his face he has always the chance of righting himself. We continually hear of their commercial integrity, which is undoubtedly very great, though not springing from any innate principles of fair-dealing but from a desire to save face. I have very little doubt but that a Chinese merchant would immediately "do" you if he could be perfectly sure of not being found out, and so losing face, and that too without in any way violating his own feelings. "Face," or otherwise "appearances," is a Chinaman's passport to respectability, and therefore of great commercial value, but has nothing whatever to do with the hidden principles of honour and morality. That honesty pays better than dishonesty is a fact well known and firmly adhered to by merchants in a large way of business. To those in a small way of business, honesty does not pay, and consequently does not exist, but instead ability in squeezing is accepted as the gauge of capacity.

The first essential in dealing with Chinese is control of temper. I do not mean that one should not possess a temper, on the contrary, it is a distinct advantage to have one, only it must be kept well in hand. A man of irritable, rasping temperament quickly loses respect and weakens control, while he who can keep calm under any circumstances, and only very rarely gives rein to a fierce outburst at the psychological moment, invariably compels admiration and obedience, for, it is reasoned, if a man who has command of his temper gets angry it is because he has just cause, and the fault must necessarily lie with those who call his anger forth.

Under no circumstances, except in actual self-defence, strike a Chinaman. The pain or insult it may cause him is as nothing in comparison with the lowering effect it will have on your own status in native eyes. From being well-considered you will at once become an object of contemptuous dislike.

The empire of China is considerably larger than the whole of Europe, contains limitless natural resources, and is inhabited by a hardy race of some four hundred million souls who are bound together by ties of blood, language, tradition and religion. This race, which until quite modern times existed as a world apart and was sufficient unto itself in all things, is highly developed both mentally and physically, though its government, as judged by Western ideas, is hopelessly obsolete.

If left to themselves I see no reason why the Chinese should not slumber on as they now are till the crack of doom, but, the world having become so reduced in size through the agencies of steam and electricity, they never will again be left undisturbed, but more and more subjected to the pressure of other nationalities in the feverish struggle for domination and wealth. To this pressure they will surely yield in one way or another. Will they forestall the inevitable by reforming themselves, or will they for a time fall beneath the foreign yoke until they have learnt their lesson, and then reassert their solidarity and independence?

In whatever light we may view these people or animadvert on their numberless contradictory qualities and failings, it is as certain as day and night that they are here to stay, if only by force of numbers, and that no political convulsions will wipe them out. They may be battered and even sundered for a time, but each successive shock will only serve to resuscitate their vitality.

Already possessing an equipment of wealth, numbers, thrift, good physique and high mental power, they only await good government to start them along the rails of progress. Whatever nations may rise or fall, the future is big with promise for the children of Han.

* * * * *

Roughly, the mandarin or official language is spoken by all officials throughout the empire and by all classes in those provinces which lie north of the Yangtse, while south of this line Cantonese is the principal dialect, although the number of others is legion, and so pronounced are the differences between them that countrymen dwelling but a few miles apart are frequently at a loss to understand each other.

On one occasion, when making "a little trip to Japan," I took my Pekingese boy with me. Having missed the fortnightly mail-boat I made the passage from Chefoo in a small German collier, and on arrival at Nagasaki took rickshas to the hotel. In the streets were a goodly number of Chinese, members of a considerable colony of small traders, and the sight of compatriots in a foreign land greatly delighted the boy, who, on my departure after tiffin to make a tour of the town, asked if he meanwhile might go out to drink tea with his countrymen. I gave permission, but on returning some hours later to the hotel found him in a very disappointed frame of mind, which was accounted for by his explanation that the Chinese residents in Nagasaki were all Cantonese, and that not being able to understand a word of mandarin they had perforce been obliged to converse with each other as best they could in pidgin English. He said, "Looksee b'long all same Chinaman, no savez talkee."

The Pekingese are very discriminative and frequently condescendingly refer to all other Chinese as "outside men" or "foreigners."

Pidgin English is a queer jargon composed of a verbatim translation of Chinese sentences together with a slight admixture of Portuguese and French, the frequent wrongful substitution of similar sounding words and a lavish use of the terminals ee and o.

"S'pose you wantchee catchee olo chinaware, compradore savez talkee my," represents, "If you want to get some old chinaware your Chinese agent will let me know," while I have heard "two times twicee" for "twice two," and "last day to-night" for "last evening."

The word pidgin means work of any kind, as in "plenty pidgin" or "no got pidgin," and pidgin English simply means a workable knowledge of colloquial English as picked up by tradesmen, servants and coolies, in contradistinction to English as taught in the schools.

On the northern frontiers there is also pidgin Russian.

The written language is the same everywhere, each character, of which the Chinese say there are between eighty and a hundred thousand, representing a complete word, so that before being able to read, and more especially write, a single sentence, each individual character in it must be closely studied and committed to memory, as we commit to memory the letters of the alphabet, but with the difference that whereas the alphabet consists of but twenty-six simple letters, Chinese caligraphy contains almost a hundred thousand characters of extreme complexity.

From earliest boyhood to the grave Chinese students never cease, yet never complete, committing these characters to memory and welding them into those graceful verses and essays which are the pride of Chinese literature.

Handwriting is accounted a fine art, and for many hours each day, year in and year out, characters are laboriously copied by means of a little brush filled with ink, which in the form of a cake or stick similar to Indian ink is moistened and ground on to a stone slab or "ink-stone," until the penmanship is frequently of a firmness and beauty surpassing that of copper-plate. In such veneration is the written character held that it is accounted wrong to debase in any way paper on which writing may be inscribed, wherefore conscientious literati sometimes pass along the streets gathering into baskets stray pieces of paper bearing written characters, to burn them reverently in miniature pagodas or towers erected on public ground for that especial purpose.

The career of a student is considered to be the most honourable of all, but though chiefly restricted to handwriting, knowledge of characters, composition and national history, the Chinese admit that no man has ever yet thoroughly mastered his own language or even learnt all the characters.

How then about foreigners' knowledge of the language? It is like the nibblings of a mouse at a mountain.

In the course of two or three years a European by means of hard work, good memory and facile ear, may succeed in speaking one of the dialects so as generally to make himself understood, but to the end of his days his speech, for more than a few sentences, would never be mistaken in the dark by one Chinaman for that of another Chinaman.

As for the written character, I do not believe it possible for any European to acquire more than a superficial general, or a mature one-sided, knowledge of it. Some missionaries, notably Jesuits, have given their lives to the work and have undoubtedly attained to considerable erudition in the classics and in subjects pertaining to religious doctrines, but in place give them some business papers or other documents in current use and they would be at once hopelessly nonplussed.

A man may have mastered eight or ten thousand characters and may be able to read or dictate letters on any subject, but he probably would not be able to read a single line from most of the classics.

I have heard, as a phenomenal thing, of a foreigner being able to write a letter himself, but the fact of its being phenomenal shows how unusual it was, and does not prove the absence of either crudities or errors.

All Europeans, even the most competent, are always assisted by educated Chinamen when engaged on serious Chinese work. Unaided, they might read much correctly, but they might altogether miss the sense, and most probably would meet with characters they did not know.

As for writing, it is impossible. Even if unaided one did manage to compose anything, it would be the work of a tyro and would never pass muster with literary Chinese, while the penmanship would be laboured and coarse, for the manner of holding the pen or brush is quite different from our own, and if not acquired almost from infancy the knack comes with difficulty when bones and sinews are more firmly set.

With regard to mastering what is called the running character, which, by way of illustration, may be said to correspond to our shorthand, the thing is not to be thought of.

To apply a general test, no European would ever have the slightest chance of passing even the lowest of the literary examinations.

One may well ask what is the reason of this inability to reach the attainments of even a moderately well-educated Chinaman.

No European can give his whole time from earliest childhood to the undivided study of Chinese, and even if he could, I very much question if the unattractive nature of native literature would satisfy his more versatile brain, while the absence of social intercourse between the two races removes the greatest of all incentives to perseverance.

On the other hand, the Chinese are saturated with a hereditary instinct for their own language and literature, which instinct, besides assiduous cultivation for thousands of years, is fostered from infancy by their surroundings, and is so exactly suited to their patient, phlegmatic temperament that it comes to them as naturally as the air they breathe, and even if unable to read but a few characters in a phrase, they will arrive at the meaning as surely as a well-bred hound will follow a trail.

And so it follows that although Europeans of most brilliant intellect may devote long years and infinite labour to the study of Chinese, lacking this native instinct, they can never attain to that ripened and fluent knowledge which is a heritage of the Mongol race alone.

* * * * *

What to say anent missionaries?

In England alone the proselytising spirit is strong, and every parish subscribes liberally to missionary funds in order that labourers in the vineyard may not be wanting, and that the ends of the earth may know the tidings of joy.

Most European residents in China are adverse to missionaries and express their opinions with such vehemence as to generally obscure criticisms of a more temperate nature. According to this majority the missionaries do nothing but harm. Frequently of poor education, and lacking altogether in tact and discretion, they thrust themselves in where they are not wanted, they interfere in local matters, ignore local customs, offend local susceptibilities, and by allowing young unmarried ladies without experience and frequently without suitable escort to wander about the country, to outrage all sense of decency, thus generating ill-will which not infrequently leads to riots, bloodshed and diplomatic trouble, while the good they do is microscopic and the number of converts or "rice-Christians" coincides with the amount of alms distributed, and who, when nothing further is to be acquired, revert to the faith, or indifference, of their forefathers. Building fine residences with the funds provided by gullible folks at home, and constructing diminutive churches with the few remaining bricks, drawing fat salaries which increase pari passu with the number of their children, and taking long summer holidays in Japan or in the mountains when business men must be hard at work, nothing but condemnation is heard for the whole system which, they say, should be forcibly suppressed by the various Governments concerned.

While enough of this loud-voiced deprecation may be true to lend a colouring to the whole, I have no hesitation in saying that the opinions of most of the critics are absolutely worthless. In fact, they know nothing whatever about either the missionaries or their work, but simply repeat, with their own additions, things they have heard from any and every source without ever troubling to verify them personally. Never was there a clearer case of "giving a dog a bad name," etc.

We civilians in China frequently lead far from model lives and are in no position to throw stones, for which reason, probably, the mere sight of a professional good man is worse than the proverbial red rag, and the tendency is strong, I own, to disparage him and all his works, while serenely forgetful of our own palpable shortcomings.

I have known one or two missionaries commit shady actions. I have known several civilians commit crimes.

Missionaries, like ourselves, it must not be forgotten, are very human, and contain in their ranks men widely differing in degrees of fitness.

In various remote places I have met missionaries of many denominations-- Jesuits, Anglicans, Non-conformists, etc.--and on closer acquaintance I have almost invariably found them at heart, whatever their methods, attainments or achievements, to be men of sterling worth, of lofty ideals, leading noble, self-denying lives, and fighting the good fight for love of God and man, and for the faith that is in them.

From the militant nature of their calling they cannot avoid interesting themselves in the lives and customs of the natives, and that their message to the heathen, inviting them to forsake the gods of their fathers and embrace the only true faith, arouses hostility in the most conservative people on earth, is in no sense to be wondered at.

Of medical missionaries who found hospitals and heal the sick, as well as of those who devote their lives to teaching the blind to read and the dumb to speak, adverse comment by anyone speaking with sincerity and briefest knowledge of the facts would be impossible. These missions of mercy shine as great beacons of Christianity through the gloom of heathen darkness.

The greatest fault brought home to several missions is, in my opinion, their interference in legal quarrels between native Christians and their unconverted fellow-citizens. This interference has undoubtedly frequently occurred and with marked success, thereby causing extreme irritation to the Chinese officials, who dread possible complications with foreign consuls, and arousing the bitter resentment of the populace, not only against all Christians, but also against all foreigners.

Indiscretion and want of tact are usually the fruit of enthusiastic inexperience, for veteran missionaries have generally tempered zeal with both suavity and cautiousness.

That young, unmarried women, brought up in the pure atmosphere of Western homes and unaccustomed to the nauseous sights and insanitary surroundings of Eastern cities, should be allowed to ruin their healths, risk death by indescribable tortures, and in Chinese eyes to forfeit their reputations, for the sake of doing a very problematical amount of good is, I cannot help feeling, a great mistake and too heavy a price to pay. If there must be missionaries, at least let them be men, and it would be far better and much more in accordance with the divine will if these girls settled in some one of our many colonies, married, and gave sons to the world, who then in due time might take up the cross of missionary endeavour.

On the whole, I should say that while missionaries are greatly over-condemned by Europeans residing in China, the good they do is over-estimated by people at home.

Putting aside all criticism of missionaries themselves, the vital question is-- "Will they succeed in converting China to Christianity?"

I am not sufficiently versed in the necessary statistics to offer a very valuable opinion, but, such as it is, it tends to the conviction that they will not.

It is a mistake to believe that persecution is an unfailing help to a religious cause. It is so only when the persecution is sporadic and fitful: storms succeeded by sunshine. When persecution partakes of a stern, unrelenting nature, such as has recently been meted out to Chinese converts, it certainly destroys, or at least stultifies, growth.

Despite remonstrances from the great Powers and despite all treaties, I greatly fear that these persecutions will be more bitter and more general in the future than they have been in the past.

While the progress of conversion is thus delayed and Christianity by drawing the fire of hate and intolerance absorbs all attention, Mohammedanism is silently making considerable strides, favoured by a period of bright sunshine, and unless storms of persecution soon burst again to roll back the tide, as after the last Mohammedan rising, when, it is said, loads of human ears were forwarded to Peking in token of successful repression, followers of the Prophet bid fair to establish a position in China which cannot be coerced and must be recognised, and which would oppose to Christianity an even stronger and keener influence than is exerted now.

I have often heard the question asked--"Would the Chinese be any the better for becoming Christians?" and the reply has usually been that they would not.

Personally, I believe that Christianity would supply the Chinaman's character with an element which it now altogether lacks--chivalry, and which, added to his many excellent qualities, would place him in the very forefront of the peoples of this earth.

If China accepted Christianity her moral and material regeneration would be assured, stagnation would yield to progress, darkness to light and hostility to friendliness. Instead of the unwieldy mass now lying sulking at the feet of other nations, China would become a strong, self-reliant, prosperous state, fearing none, but held in respect and friendship by all.

Heathen China may possibly fall under the yoke of foreign powers, but the spirit of Christianity, bringing with it reformation and progress, having once been breathed into her nostrils, it would be just as possible to chain the waters of the ocean as to hold her in lasting bondage, and Christian China would be free.

* * * * *

Forty odd years ago, at the close of the second great war, China was a veritable Eldorado for Europeans, where all turned to gold beneath the lightest touch of alien hands. Fortunes were made with startling rapidity, and money came in so freely that the standard of living amongst foreign merchants and their employ 閻 reached to such preposterous heights of luxuriousness, that when the inevitable reaction set in, want, and even ruin, supervened where plenty should have been found.

From that date to this the descent from an inflated prosperity to a mean working level has been gradual and sure.

What has been the cause of this descent?

Forty years ago the foreign trade was practically monopolised by Englishmen, who had only to place their goods on the market of any newly-opened port for them to be snapped up at almost any price by Chinese merchants, who then possessed but little knowledge of foreign wares and were exceedingly timid of their own officials. As time wore on this ignorance and timidity grew less and less, until the Chinese purchaser came to close quarters with the English importer, eliminating middlemen at the small ports and transferring operations chiefly to the great emporiums of Hongkong and Shanghai. Americans and Continentals of all nationalities arrived in rapidly-increasing numbers, bringing merchandise for the Chinese market, thus giving native buyers a much larger variety of goods from which to choose, and introducing a competition fatal to the former enormous profits.

Although the volume of both import and export trade shows a continuous yearly increase, it tends more and more to centre in the hands of a comparatively few large European firms with which Chinese merchants from all parts of the Empire directly negotiate, to the exclusion of foreigners in a small way of business.

Another reason for the decrease of profitable commercial openings is the practical extinction of China's tea trade with England, Ceylon and India now supplying the home-market, and although as great a quantity of tea is still exported from China as formerly, it nearly all goes to Russia, and this trade being in the hands of Russian monopolists, there is but little employment for other nationalities, while even here it probably will not be many years before the Russians largely follow our example in abandoning Chinese tea in preference for that of Ceylon and India.

Similarly the steam shipping, which originally was almost exclusively British-owned, is gradually passing to the credit of Chinese capitalists, if not in name yet in reality, and any new development in this line is almost sure to be mainly financed from native sources.

The opinion is largely held that accordingly as China is opened up by railways, by steam navigation on the inland waters, and by simplification of inland duties, foreigners will reap such advantages as may again enable them to quickly amass fortunes. Let there be no delusion on this point.

Wherever openings for trade occur there will instantly be found shrewd Chinese business men backed by a plentiful supply of native capital, and the Westerner will get but little that is worth having.

When the West River was thrown open to steamer traffic a few years since it was confidently predicted on all sides that it would cause a considerable development in foreign shipping. Nothing of the kind. On a recent trip to Wuchow I saw scores, and possibly hundreds, of small steamers and launches crammed with cargo and passengers, or towing strings of deep-laden junks, but they were all Chinese-owned, while the only foreign-owned vessels to be seen were a few gun-boats and less than half-a-dozen steamers, which it is generally believed barely earn enough to cover expenses.

The descent thus accounted for has chiefly then been caused by the competition amongst Westerners allowing Chinese merchants to get on even terms with them, when, being extremely good business men, holding absolute command of the native markets, and able to live much more cheaply than Europeans, they have generally ousted small foreign traders from the out-ports by carrying operations over their heads direct to well-known houses at the great centres of trade.

Firms doing a large import and export business should prosper, although harassed by continual fluctuations in the value of silver, but their prosperity will redound to the direct advantage of a few only, while the chances of a man who comes out from home with a small capital being able to make for himself a successful commercial career are woefully meagre. Even representatives of wealthy syndicates, after investigating prospects on the spot, generally come to the conclusion that capital can be more profitably invested elsewhere than in China.

On the other hand there are a considerable number of official appointments to be obtained, carrying with them comfortable remuneration, but these are mostly filled up in England and in the several countries concerned.

Professional men, such as doctors, lawyers and dentists, working both for Chinese clients and foreign residents, have capital opportunities, while for captains, officers and engineers for steamers, engineers and directors for docks and factories, professors for various colleges, mining experts and railroad constructors, there is an increasing demand at fair salaries, but, considering the trying climate, the banishment from home and the persistent decline in the value of silver, residence in the Far East, even on a large income, is a doubtful advantage.

The collapse of silver has been so great that whereas twenty or thirty years ago four silver dollars would purchase a sovereign, and a salary of four hundred dollars a month represented twelve hundred pounds a year, now it takes more than twelve dollars to purchase a sovereign, so that a similar salary of four hundred dollars a month represents less than four hundred pounds a year.

It is a common belief at home that fluctuations in the value of silver are not felt when purchases are confined to a silver-using country. This is quite a mistake. China is a silver-using country, yet the standard of value maintained by her four hundred million souls is neither silver nor gold but copper cash, and the ultimate cost of everything of native origin is regulated by its value in cash.

A coolie's wages a few years ago may have been six thousand cash a month, and a dollar being then purchasable for say a thousand cash, you gave him six dollars a month. To-day his wages may still be six thousand cash but a dollar being now worth only five hundred cash, you are obliged to give him twelve dollars a month. Precisely the same rule applies to meat, coals, vegetables, etc.

For all imported foreign articles, such as clothes, stores, wines, etc., you must give enough in silver dollars to make up the price as reckoned at home, that is, in gold, and as you now have to give three times as many dollars for a sovereign as formerly your imported goods are three times dearer, or, in other words, the value of silver has fallen and its purchasing power is very much less than it used to be the whole world over.

For a man drawing his salary in dollars the cost of living in the Far East is more than double what it was twenty-five years ago. For those who direct big businesses the earnings of which are in silver and the expenses largely in gold, as well as for those who had already invested their fortunes in shares prior to the utter collapse of silver, the past few years have been a period of crushing losses, while the future must be fraught with grave anxiety.

In short, but few fortunes are to be made in China, while money is very easily lost, and unless a man before leaving home secures a definite position in a good business firm, in Government employ or in some profession, it would be most unwise of him to go out on the chance of finding employment after his arrival.

THE END

www.ingramcontent.com/pod-product-compliance
Lightning Source LLC
Chambersburg PA
CBHW070104300526
45788CB00016B/2240